How to Find and Keep a

BMW

Black Man Working

by
Julia Hare

The Black Think Tank

How to Find and Keep a
BMW
Black Man Working

ISBN: 0-9613086-6-4

Price: $10.00

Published by: **THE BLACK THINK TANK**
1801 Bush Street, Suite 118
San Francisco, California 94109
(415) 474-1707

Dedication

To all my sisters

and

the many BMWs

waiting in the wings

CONTENTS

Getting Ready To Kick It

Whenever black women get together, you can almost always hear them crying "ain't no black men out here." "Ain't nothing on these streets, child." "Where're all the good black men—they're either married, gay or playing games." And if you live in a small town, "Girlfriend" will tell you you can just about hang it up.

Just the other day, I attended the funeral of a close friend's father. After the ceremony, we walked out of the mortuary and stood on the sidewalk to wait for the procession to pass by. In a few minutes, a sister came up and asked us, "where are the men?" She said she knew the corpse in the coffin was the body of an old man in his seventies but that she was there in the hope that, inasmuch as he lived the sporting life, somebody or "something" young enough for her might show up at the funeral.

Many are the times when sisters are meeting on very serious issues — say, saving the black child, or social liberation, whether the tragedy in Somalia, South Africa, Rwanda or wherever, multicultural diversity or Aristide's return to Haiti — the conversation will suddenly switch with no warning to "the black male shortage".

Where have all the black males gone? A lot of sisters are afraid they've been looking in all the wrong places. Many have no trouble bumping into men who appear to be eligible if not elegant catches. It's just that when they do, it always turns out something's wrong.

They say, too many brothers are "threatened" by successful black women. Or, they're already taken or they ain't the marrying

1

kind, you know. With some you go to bed and wake up to find their wrist is limp.

Recently, in the middle of an annual black bourgeoisie hen's party around Christmas time in San Francisco, a prominent black woman stood up and said she already knew exactly why she hadn't been able to find a black man.

Everybody said "why?"

"Cause I scare they ass away," the sister bragged, slipping easily into the vernacular middle class black people use when they want to "get down" or bask in being black for dramatic effect. "The first thing I let them niggers know is they got to show me a negative HIV and a positive cash flow." One hefty lady — with the confidence that can come with middle age — claimed she already "buried one husband, divorced one, lived with a third, and I don't want no mo' runover shoes beneath my bed."

"What about his false teeth in the Efferdent in your china cups?" another quipped. "Yeah, I tell them, if you want to be with me, you got to have a J.O.B."

And so it went into the night. "Yeah Girl, I can have nothing with nobody all by myself."

When the laughter died, a grim but sophisticated claque of stylish corporate sisters inched over to where I was sitting and told me they knew of my longstanding collaboration with my husband at the Black Think Tank in the movement to mend black male/female relationships. Under the privacy of the moment, they broke down and pleaded for help and comfort in the rawest language they could call up to describe the inner pain they felt. They bared many

2

moving recollections of the joyless days and nights they'd spent in quiet but unending desperation. One confessed she had adorned a disguise and gone into an adult store for a dildo, vibrator and batteries. They begged me to tell them the secrets of finding a good black man — a working black man.

They wanted to know if the problem was one of simply looking in the wrong places for something which, in the first place, isn't there or anywhere else. Or whether they set their standards too high — or too low.

I saw that one sister seemed to be hanging back, but as soon as she could catch me alone, she came over and tried to remind me of a seminar I once presented. She said she remembered I had made the point that it seems black women don't mind telling one another the most intimate private inside details when they are looking for a job or trying to find a better condo or a car, but can't be very open in their search for a man.

If looking for an apartment, they'll say, "if you see anything, let me know, and don't put me in any ol' part of town. I want a pretty good zip code, Honey." They'll even ask about the price and the place to find a special dress. But when it comes to looking for a man, the one they hope to share the rest of their lives with, they don't want to ask for fear of exposing some shameless vulnerability.

On the way home from that hen's party, I decided if Michael Jordan can write a book called "How to Keep from Getting AIDS," somebody ought to be able to tell a sister how to find and keep a good enough man. I called the sister and said I'd write a book on "How to Find and Keep a BMW (Black Man Working)."

In the process, I'll enter a lot of forbidden places, harbor no secrets, in the exposure and examination of the ways and motivations of the dwindling supply of marriageable black men — especially the marrying kind.

Once we've told how to find one, we'll get into how to know what, if anything, a brother has to offer a woman. We'll also keep in mind its connection to all we've learned about what black women want in a man. So brothers, you can pick up something too.

Not that it'll be easy. The supply keeps dwindling, even as we write. On top of that, it sometimes seems that everybody — and I mean everybody — wants a piece of the black man, if not a black man working. He's on everybody's most wanted list.

One of the reasons, in fact, that the supply keeps dwindling is because the white woman keeps raiding the barn. Their man shortage isn't as great as ours, especially at the top — and only about one or two percent would ever marry a black man — but the white woman outnumbers us ten to one. So when two percent of them comes over for "the big rip-off," that's one-fifth of the brothers gone.

The white woman wants the cream of the crop. So, since she's twice as likely to be a college graduate as the black male is, she puts a bigger hurting on the already limited and dwindling black male supply — especially at the top. In fact she'll want a college brother even when she didn't get out of the 8th grade herself, figures show.

But leaving the white woman aside (just for the moment), it's now being said in some circles that the white man also wants a piece of the black man. Sisters, who deserve a piece of the brother, cling to the quest for their share of any remainders — and sometimes finds she's left with only a piece, if that — and a piece of a black man, as in a piece of a car, is likely to be something broken down and sometimes whipped down also.

Problem is, sisters no longer want to settle for a piece of a broken down brother. They want a brand new dream. After a while you get tired of patching up old transmissions, brakes and batteries. One thing breaks down, here comes another, something else is wrong. That's why when we come home in the evening, before we speak, especially if the brother is grinning or trying to do something nice, we say "What's wrong now? What'd you do this time?"

What does the black woman want from the black man? Maybe too much. But, the bottom line is we want a brother with a job of his own. It's not that we're all that mercenary, though it may seem that way. You have to understand that a brother with a job is more likely to be emotionally stable, at least enough to hold it, have a better looking supply of clothes, a minimum of intelligence, overall savvy — commitment and general socialization. Not somebody we're going to have to raise all over — and get accused of being domineering or "matriarchal" or "castrating" to boot — before we can have a satisfactory love relation with someone we can call our own. Besides, you don't have to have a job to be considered a woman in this society, but you have to be employed to be considered a man.

So, hold your horses, we're putting every brother on notice, from this day forward, what we want is a BMW (a Black Man Working). We can handle the rest.

The white woman may want a whole lot more. They scope for a high profile brother, or at least a brother with a high profile job, a position, maybe a corporate executive with his own expense account, trips to Africa, Europe and all the perks. I've heard of white women who don't even want to take trips with a brother unless he's the U.S. Ambassador to wherever they're going. And she expects the royal treatment long before she boards the boat.

So far as she's concerned, there's always the star-level entertainer, the bigtime athlete. They want the high life of the all-pro ball player, O.J. Simpson style, and the tragedy and mystery of double murder isn't likely to change that. In fact, a recent poll showed that three out of four women would still date him. Long before the trial, two-thirds of the white public already pegged O.J. as guilty. Funny thing, you rarely see a white athlete at the top of his game walking down the street (or aisle) with a black woman. Wonder why?

Brothers, listen, I know all of you aren't guilty, but you're going to have to teach your rainbow brethren that their mothers were black. They were born black, and chances are they will die black.

Can you imagine, leaving all his melanin enriched sisters? I mean, brothers fresh out of the projects, where they learned their basketball moves, the dunk, which got them out of the slow-learners classes and, barely out of college, but suddenly have the nerve to stand up and say before the whole white world that they've out-grown black women. Wilt Chamberlain, Reggie Jackson, O.J. Simpson, and Brent Staples, to name a few. Not just athletes, this thing includes the movie idols and the entertainers. Where do we begin if we wanted to name them? Then, as soon as they get in trouble with the white folks, they come running to black people and Minister Farrakhan. Michael Jackson, who got clobbered for pouring affections on a white boy, not caring to give his tremendous generosity of gifts and the advantages of multi-thousand dollar toys to black boys and girls, even had the nerve to pick a white woman, jump

6

heterocentric and get married. Low and behold, there she is, Elvis Presley's daughter. Her father stole our music (remember Big Mabel Thornton) and the daughter steals the "man."

Being closer to the corporate ways (even if often at the bottom rung), we still get a chance to learn and take the best from everybody, as when we had to scuffle between keeping up our slave quarters and the master's mansion on the plantation, we know the ways of the corporation. We know how to go after what we want in the white mainstream. We can plan our own promotions — and get them if we have a chance — even without sleeping with the boss on a par with the white woman, even without bending over or folding up like too many brothers do. We can plan our budgets, pinch off and feed our children from a little or nothing tucked in our bra, or wherever. But, sisters, you have to start to learn that the same kind of energy, the same hawkeyed attention, has to be brought into our repertoire when we're looking to find and keep a good black man (our unsuspecting BMW).

Why are we reluctant to set clear goals in the arena of life the way we do in the pursuit of material objects and acquisitions? It probably goes back to some kind of thinking that "marriages are made in Heaven," so we think it's wrong to set a blueprint on the brother who could be our natural (or supernatural) partner. Maybe we don't want to think of our chosen one as any kind of targeted quarry.

That's why I just had to do this book. At the Black Think Tank, we've studied and talked with every kind of man that's still out there. If you want an Afrocentric nationalist, we've got a good case study. If you prefer a Eurocentric assimilationist (a "coconut") we have an enormous laboratory of subjects. If you desire the polygamous brother, read on and find out how to coexist in his harem

7

(my husband says "hare-em," but he knows not to look, let alone to touch).

Maybe you always wanted a Mr. T or a Minister Khalid. If so, these pages hold the secret to winning a baldheaded brother's heart. If your older man doesn't have the energy to keep you up or keep up with you, socially or/and sexually, maybe you should slow down before you look for the younger brother. But if you should find yourself still kicking it with a younger man, through no fault of your own, by hook or by crook, relax, it's all right, no problem. If you want a younger man, I say *train what you want.*

Speaking of youth, let me say a special word to my college sisterfriends. When I visit campuses around the country lecturing on Black Male/Female Relationships and The Black Family, I can see the stress, the distress, as well as the mistress (and mistresses) registered all over your innocent faces. One sophomore at the University of Michigan's Ann Arbor campus confessed to me that she had arrived at a reluctant conclusion. When I asked her what it was, she said that the brothers with the scholarships playing ball actually think that a white woman goes with the scholarship. I said "you don't mean it," but I had to admit that it sometimes seems to be the case.

Still no need to dash your hopes. When you finish reading this handbook, you'll know how to select and groom your own private MVP (Most Valuable Player), if you know what I mean.

Even if your thing is for the history-minded brother and you hope somehow to reincarnate your own, you might learn how to make it work. Maybe it's not as hard as staying with a contemporary Carter G. Woodson, a high-tech Booker T Washington (the brother who wants to go into business for himself, who preaches selfhelp but settles with helping himself to what you have). But if you find yourself in love with one of these "self-starters," there's a section on why you should keep your job while the enterprise is getting off the ground and how to hold your sisterfriends at bay once his business starts to bloom.

You'll learn how to watch Girlfriend closely, very carefully. Don't let her fool you, with such friendly rhetoric as: "Child, I wouldn't take this, I wouldn't take that." because when you begin to restrict yourself to a man with a J.O.B. (though he may not treat you with the same respect and tender loving care as the less marketable self starter), the very girlfriend admonishing you most to leave the man you're with will have her slippers on your side of the bed before you can sign another lease.

If you're working in a corporation, I know you're running into many brothers who claim (at least when they're in compromising positions) that they want a successful black woman. They'll even tell you they like a woman who's strong and independent, irregardless of success. Okay, but careful, don't you be no fool. Wonder why so many successful sisters are without successful black men who can operate on an even keel in a romantic relationship? We'll get to the bottom of that.

On the other hand, get ready to meet and greet the black man, if you haven't already, who will boast that he wants his woman to be able to pass the "paper bag and blow test" (lighter than a paper bag, with blow hair). What do you do if you can't meet the paper bag and blow test, at least not quite?

How do you handle the brother, clearly moving on in age if not in consciousness of kind, who constantly seeks a woman young enough to be his daughter instead of you. First thing you know, he could be backing right into the arms of your daughter. You could wind up sharing your bed and STD (socially transmitted disease) with your daughter's boy friend, if you aren't hip.

I'll dissect among other things, the brother who thinks that Mother's Day is the first of every month. A lot of sisters mistakenly think this type of brother comes under the exclusive domain of the welfare woman. They have a lot to learn. Better watch your paycheck, Miss School Teacher, Ms. Sales Rep., Ms. Middle Manager, Ms. Other Woman (and some *Mrs. Other Women*) married sisters following the a la carte approach to "man-sharing" proposed several years ago by Howard University counselor Audrey Chapman. Better get hipped to the "Sweetheart Swindle," so you can recognize it when it comes your way. Otherwise, the next Sweetheart Swindle victim could be you.

So read on young lady, and be ready for the brother who approaches you with visions of polygamy or pseudo-polygamy which he proposes to practice on you. Or, when your man suddenly decides polygamy could be the answer to your prayers and his — as soon as you catch him with his pants down, he wiggles out of the situation telling you, "this is the key to what the black race needs."

If you're getting tired of brothers who continue to cling to the blonde hair syndrome — because "women are women, love is love, sex is sex" — yet take special pains to avoid being seen with anybody that looks like their own black mother, we need to talk.

Have you heard about all of the sisters who are tired and worried about the snowballing cases of brothers who are "bi-sexual," or openly gay? Worse, it appears their marriage rate is soaring on the backs of desperate sisters given to denial. These brothers will hide in the closet flexing pump iron muscles with their hooks in you (their social cover) then leave you and three kids in the crib for their new male crush.

How to Find and Keep a BMW can be a veritable flashlight for finding your way around in the tricky dimness of the black male shortage. It can be your secret weapon, but let's keep it the black woman's secret. There are people who, when they see you with a good thing, will want to steal it or take it away. It's okay to discuss it at a private party, but you might hesitate to take it to the office to be shared with "the girls" because as soon as 10,000 others discover the existence of your gold mine, somebody is liable to get there before you do.

Without airing all our secrets, or yours, come with me to all the hidden places as we scale the depths and heights of the dwindling supply of marriageable (and marrying) brothers. Let's learn more of the art of determining what, if anything, a given black man has to offer a serious-mined black woman like you. We'll base a lot of our insights on what we've learned about what it is that black women want from a man. That way, brothers, you can pick up something too.

The Successful Black Woman Syndrome

There's a war going on, a war of harsh words and animosity, between black women and black men. It's threatening to break out into open political conflict and escalated black male/female chaos. Within this overall war is the explosive battle of the so-called "strong black woman" and the not-so-successful black man, the kind of man she's too often forced to settle for, or have nobody at all.

But finding all too quickly, in too many cases, the loneliness she hadn't quite reckoned on, plus the social stigma of being alone or without a man, many sisters can't understand why, even when they lower their requirements in a man, they have picked up another problem. They regret their inability to raise the aspirations of the men they meet. On top of that, they find that either the men feel threatened by them and constantly jockey for position in the relationship, or shy away. At other times, they get together with the men but don't know how to make the men who seem to have given up on their ambitions want to get ahead in life the way they do.

The tumult is escalating to the point where it's threatening to break out in open, collective male/female strife on top of the individual disaffection and the silent, seething black male/female disidence. In certain circumstances where a black woman may be promoted to a high position in a local company, or has a chance to run for high office in the town, to become a city official, the principal of a school, or whatever token top position that may be out there, the sister is finding herself lined up not only against the white status quo but the black male contention as well. Some are now saying their biggest battle is with the black man.

Word just came, even as I write, from a very trustworthy

sister in San Diego, California, where a black woman supposedly has or had the chance to become a high-ranking police official, but a group of black men objected, going so far as to say they'd rather see a white man there instead of a black woman. It seems these brothers believe that it is the successful black woman who is taking the job they think they ought to have.

When the men and women actually sat down together to talk about the situation, a black woman told the men, "you think you're in some kind of war now, you're on the verge of inviting murder because, if we did step down or step aside for you black men, you'd get the job but the first thing you'd do is slink over and marry a white woman."

This scenario, according to other sources, is happening in Georgia, in Chicago, in Oakland, in Washington, D.C. (which recently witnessed a bitter battle between Marion Barry and Sharon Pratt) and all across the Diaspora, wherever black men and women meet. Sadly, it's all because of being caught in between somebody else's agenda and our own, plus putting personal gain above the interests of the race, topped off by misplaced rage.

Not surprisingly — and this is a part of the problem and the source of much of her passion — as the black woman mounts these new positions, the higher up she gets, she finds that there are no black men available. Across a widening sexual chasm, a lot of brothers are starting to say that the black woman is too strong, and sisters counter with the cutting conclusion that the black man is too weak.

The black man believes that the black woman is taking the job that a black man ought to get, which his woman at home and society at large expects of him. Although there's at least an element of truth in that, these men fail to realize that even if it is true in part, of far greater significance is the jobs the white woman is getting.

And so, instead of confronting the white man, the black woman reaches out to share what the black man has, while the black man squabbles with the black woman over what she gets. Rather than confront the white man, or the white woman for that matter, the black man directs his resentment toward the black woman. The black woman should confront the powers-that-be for more of the jobs that white women get, and the black man should be fighting the white man, demanding more jobs for the race instead of fighting with the black woman over token positions.

Having no power to share, as things now stand, and unable to outtalk his woman on an individual level in the majority of cases, the black man faces her with little to fight with beyond the physical. Additionally, his predicament is complicated by the fact that, on a deep unconscious level, he is dealing in part with unresolved conflicts with his mother as well as "the white man's system" as he hassles with his mate.

I can say one thing, if we don't get to the bottom of this, we're headed for more confusion, division, diversion, disruption and inner turmoil than we could ever imagine. Maybe we should start by deciding, once and for all, what a strong black woman is.

Is a strong black woman one who's hung onto a good job from 9 to 5 she may or may not love? Is a strong black woman the sister who bravely stayed at her home to raise her children, fearing the public schools? Or maybe you think the strong black woman is a weight lifter, or at least a bodybuilder who can hoist a barbell above her head. Is it the knife-wielding sister who slings hash in the truckers coffee stop, bragging to her co-workers that she may be wearing a black eye from her fight with her boyfriend the night before — but they should see how she "duked the dude." Is it Robin Given's mother, Ruth Roper, who got into trouble when, using her son-in-law Mike Tyson, she was changing the economic face of boxing, switching managers from the one-third cut (sometimes 50 percent or more, down to 20 percent with regular bookkeeping records and accounting? Is it a Harlem sister raising six children alone on AFDC? Is it Angela Davis, Maya Angelou, Betty Shabazz, Queen Mother Moore, or Marion Berry's new wife, the university president's wife who only pours tea?

Maybe the strong black woman could be the Sunday School superintendent, or the public school teacher who takes no flack from so-called "at risk" children or their parents. Some might say the strong black woman is the sister who survived a prison sentence for a crime of murder, robbery or mayhem, or escaped like Asata Shakur. Funny thing is, whatever your definition, you probably think you're one. Stranger still, if you canvassed most black men, they'd generally say they'd love to have a strong black woman.

I know a lot of sisters — and probably you do too — who've come through a turbulent relationship, some divorced some now separated. The first thing they do is try to explain the breakup: "I was strong and he didn't want anything." Sure, this could be denial, but there's no denying the fact that at this moment in our history we've come face to face to what we might call *"The Successful Black Woman Syndrome"* (SBWS) — in epidemic proportions.

I mean it's getting serious. So let me tell you how to recognize it in case you yourself might have SBWS.

First let me say that Successful Black Woman Syndrome is connected as much to the man you love as anything inside of you or your psyche, just as in the case of the Battered Woman's Syndrome, it takes more than one to tango. Bear in mind that you can have SBWS without being successful just as you can be successful or even exhibit symptoms of SBWS without developing or coming down with the full-blown malady.

But I more often find the Successful Black Woman's syndrome in the psyche of the sister who's known to be an upwardly mobile go-getter. She's one who probably made it through college (we won't say how), passed all the screenings for a corporate position, and is now "one of the team." You can find her in any field, not just private industry. She could be in government or she could be a private bootstrap (if not, bra-straps) entrepreneur.

Never mind the sister's merits, or demerits (obviously her merits are likely to be many) and she has material acquisitions you could envy. Not only a chicken in every pot and a car in every garage (the company car and her own). She has a condo with a good mailing address, wears the latest designer clothes — at least when she's not expressing her identity in ethnic duds (sometimes saving her wardrobe on the sly). I mean this sister's in Armani, Chanel, Valentino, Gucci, Linda Richards trench coats and even St. John knits (if she's stayed away from the ham hocks). They buy clothes they see in the windows of Neiman Marcus (newer markups) — just because they have the disposable dough.

I can tell you the sister may be into civil rights, but it's generally going to be limited to lifetime memberships in the NAACP and the Urban League. She may even boast that they're "old and established" (the lineage factor). She may be active with her local alumni, if it's a prestigious school; but she saves the best of her social energy for her sorors. Wouldn't think of missing her weekly bridge group the Links or Jack and Jill (some of these SBWS are fast becoming tokens in the white Junior League or the League of Women Voters), or whatever highbrow social group she can get in that screens prospective members the ones where one person can keep you out and you never know why. One of these groups kept a sister out because she ran for state senator and one of the older established members was her opponent. Because the sister won a seat in the state legislature, she was blackballed. Never occurred to the group that the sister could have been a great asset to their group politically and socially, especially since they're always on the make looking for a grant to assist the "disadvantaged black girls."

The sister with SBWS leaves no perk uncovered. Expense accounts she pads to boost her reimbursements and cruises once every two years at least. She still has to learn to live with the reality that the higher she climbs, the more she personally achieves, the greater her chances of suffering acute consequences of the dwindling marriageable black male pool.

She also may quickly discover that too many of our upper-middle-class brothers are inclined to exploit their scarcity, as if they were messiahs sent here to service the over-abundant supply of strong black women. Sooner or later, our SBW comes to the unequivocal realization that the black men on her "level" exist in very limited supply. You have to understand that, from childhood, she's been taught to "marry up," to attract some man with an equal, preferably better, social class position and overall financial attainment.

What they didn't tell her, or couldn't know when she was growing up, is that in the mid-1990s (as we once wrote in *The Black Collegian*), there's an extra black female for every two black males graduating from college. This is a reality that may place her in a category where the marriageable male may elude her. On top of that, a man is freer to marry down, so she may have to compete with the beauty and personal sexual appeal of sisters in the classes below her own.

Add to this fact that we are now facing the teeming multitudes of imprisoned white collar black males (most often connected to drug abuse in some manner). The so-called drug war (and its passion for prison-building fed by mandatory sentencing policies) is linking up with "three-strikes-you're out" legislation to take a heavy toll on the marriageable black male supply, including many with college educations. Like our men, black women don't have a mindset independent of white control, don't do our own thinking, and don't really confront the system to demand hospitals instead of prisons for brothers and sisters who're addicted.

We may actually help compound things, unknowingly, when we join white agendas criminalizing our men's behavior in harsh new ways, where the cure is worse than the disease and doesn't really help that much, if at all. For instance, sexual harassment (after Clarence Thomas), date rape (after Mike Tyson) and domestic violence (since O.J. Simpson). But Senator Packwood is still in the Senate. Joe De Bartolo, owner of the San Francisco 49ers, was accused of domestic violence for a hot minute following the sports broadcast on the late night news, but this was quickly quelled. Not to mention Senator Kennedy and Chappaquiddick and his nephew, William Kennedy Smith, who was accused of rape but is now practicing medicine. Yet, Mike Tyson remains in the pen and Michael Jackson's career has been put on hold while many Roman Catholic priests with similar charges of child molestation continue to hear confessions.

We've got to stop letting others, bearing frankincense and myrrh, come between us and our men — and our men do too.

Mirror, Mirror, On The Wall. . .

You'd think that by now — here we are going into the 21st century, and we hate to admit it — but this thing about light skin and the whole color thing is still rampant in the black community. It's amazing how we talked about Michael Jackson and his sister, Latoya, for having their cosmetic surgery, then on top of that to have their skins bleached. Wonder how many black folks might have done the same thing if they could have afforded it? Especially with bleaching cream sales at an alltime high. At least Michael said it was vertiligo, this thing where your skin begins to lighten uncontrollably, to your own horror. But if that had been the case, he could have had something done to darken the light spots just as he used something to lighten the dark spots.

If the color thing is a problem for Michael, it's really hard on black women, where it starts in the womb. As soon as the baby comes out, there'll be people who'll go to the hospital room and wonder sometimes aloud, "who'd the baby take color after?" Even before marriage, some people will tell their girls, "watch who you marry because your children may come out black." They urge them to "keep it light."

This complex of light skin and dark skin starts banging the girl on the head and slapping her in the face as early as the kindergarten, where she gets her first acquaintance with not being the one that's chosen. When the teacher casts for "Cinderella," Cinderella is usually the lightskinned girl, and the dark girl is the stepmother or the wicked stepsister. When they do "The Three Bears," the light child is Goldilocks and the dark one is one of the three bears. Children's readers still portray Jill in "Jack and Jill" as very blonde. (In the sense that truth is said to be stranger than fiction and art imitates life, the preeminent black middle class children's organizaton — formed to give black middle class children educational and social vision — is named "Jack and Jill.")

Although it was quite some time ago, when the first black "Greek" sorority, Alpha Kappa Alpha, was founded at Howard University early in this century, the so-called "paper bag test" was used to blackball darker sisters. This situation soon provoked the founding of another sorority, Delta Sigma Theta, for a darker variety of sisters in opposition to AKA's early high-yellow prerequisites. When the Zeta Phi Beta sorority was founded, it became the sanctuary of the coffee colored. Although the exceptions to this categorization have increased in recent years, it is still possible to gain a rough impression of the sorority affiliation of a black woman by noticing her color and related social elements of caste and class.

Even with all the back-to-Africa movement and talk of Africa and ancient Egypt, we still hear people, even in the movement, say "she's lightskinned, but that ugly stick (meaning African features) hit her. Or, if she's lightskinned and "unattractive," you'll hear them say "that's just a lot of yellow going to waste."

On the other hand, an attractive dark sister recently told me that several brothers have said to her, "you're attractive for a dark woman." An attractive blue-black friend says a brother told her, meaning to compliment her, that "you're a goodlooking woman, and you could get ahead faster if you said you were from Africa (instead of African-American)."

I know some of you will say we're airing our dirty linen in public, but I told you this is an in-house book, this is *our* secret. Most of the linen's already hanging out anyway, every day. Everybody sees it but us. White people gloat daily at the black guests on network talk shows boasting that "I don't hate black men," or the caption underneath another will say "looking for a white man." A prominent black female elected official recently told me that it's easier to say you're *looking* for a white man than that you've *found* one. The white men aren't rushing to marry black women as much as some black women seem to think. She said even in her six figure crowd, white men may come over to wink occasionally, but they're not marrying, rushing in, where black men fear to tread.

Long before the wave of television talk shows, white people from sociology and psychology professors to army soldiers would chuckle about the apparent preference for lightskinned black women on black magazine covers. There was also a clear tendency to have the woman in a black magazine ad lighter than the man. By the late 1960s, you could see the visible trend from lightskinned beauty queens to a more multi-colored, even dark, variety. However, the old trend is reappearing in the MTV-style rap video and "blaxploitation" movies, as we drift back toward lightness in the age of "rainbow" politics and the "crossover" imperative in music and media fare.

However, when it comes to black women, the stigma of "ugliness" goes beyond the matter of color to any and all identifiably African features such as full lips, wide noses and other facial features. Whereas African tribes differ in their ideals of physical beauty — some preferring slim, round bodies, some full figures; some wanting pendulous breast, others strong thighs; some supple ankles, others fleshy; some preferring plaited hair, some completely shorn — while female ornamentation and scarification of one variety or another appears to be universal and worldwide — there is a considerable clash of culture between the European disdain for full buttocks and the African tendency to circular, even protruding hips, all the way to steatopygia (swelled buttocks).

Beyond that is the African attraction to the fat woman (growing out of the more agrarian condition of the African and the African-American) that flies in the face of the European ideal of the barebones skeletal frame exhibited by high tech commercial boardwalk models. Many black women now attempt to approximate the white woman's more flat-hipped anatomy, unwittingly misled to denigrate and diminish one of their best attributes in the minds of black men. On the other hand, more and more black men have fallen into the breast fetish more becoming to the white man's perception than the preference of the black man, who traditionally has been a hip man, even when he isn't "hipped." Some sisters have complained of boyfriends and husbands who have asked them to get breast implants!

Considering this assimilation to the white ideals of beauty, it's easy to see the pain of the sisters portrayed by Prof. Regina Turner, of Ohio's Bowling Green State University, in an article called "The Sexual Ordeal of the 'Ugly' Black Woman," which the Black Think Tank published in its *Black Male/Female Relationships* journal in the winter of 1982. Prof. Regina observed an "ugly-beautiful continuum" by which black women are thought to be judged. From childhood on up, the black woman hears — even from her own family and friends — such psychological karate chops as: "Lawd, you sho' is one mo ugly child." Or: "you ain't much to look at but. . ."

Those who wish to "salvage some value for you," according to Prof. Turner, will couch their impressions in backhanded compliments such as: "It's a good thing you're smart." Or perhaps, 'Why couldnt' you have looked like your brother?" As a child, you may have heard the more benevolent observers reassure your mother that "she'll grow out of it" while they said of your cousin Jamillah, "you go'n have to lock her up to keep the boys away from her."

Prof. Turner watched many such girls grow up to have to

endure men "trampling over" them "to drool over some 'pretty' companion," or even to discuss with you his problems of "getting a really fine" woman." Even more poignantly, many had to endure repeated experiences of being "the last to be asked out" or "being expected to grant him whatever he asks for in gratitude for being chosen. The blacker the woman is the less feminine, less genteel, less ladylike and less eligible for the pedestal, in the minds of the average brother. She is not worthy of foreplay, just slam-bam, thank you ma'm, the rock of Gibraltor, a mule, a breeder. It's said that the dark woman gets angry quicker, is "evil," that her lips "get bigger when she gets mad," that even her hair gets nappy ("goes home in the rain").

In her tell-all autobiography, *Laughing in the Dark*, Washington *Post* reporter, Patrice Gaines, was able to rescue herself from heroin addiction and "an entanglement with a series of troubled men" (including a saxophonist who forced her to engage in group sex, a hustler who beat her with a horsewhip and a 60-year-old married executive who stopped giving her money when, "riddled with shame, she stopped putting out") only when she stopped hating "my crooked, buck teeth, my ugly right thumb I caught in a mimograph machine when I was high on marijuana."

The wife of San Francisco 49ers all-pro safety Merton Hanks, Marva Hanks, though lightskinned and attractive in a Eurocentric sense, had to wrestle with a feeling of rejection because she was 6'5" tall before she attracted the shorter 6'2" Merton's bold attention and excited his irrepressible determination to marry her. Marva named their darker daughter, first born "Maya Angelou Hanks," after the poet Maya Angelou. On the day a visitor came to their home to interview her mother, the two-year-old Maya Angelou Hanks was fretting to get back upstairs where "Snow White" was playing on the VCR.

23

After a lifetime of excruciating experiences of being picked over for lightskinned women, the deeper-hued, melanin-enriched black woman is sometimes delighted to return to a family reunion or a school reunion and see what the lightskinned football queen of her high school days has turned into now. Often she delights in noting that the lightness has faded as the queen got older, darker and out of shape.

Never having had to paint her face that much in her youth, the fairer skinned girl never learned it in the many complex and necessary ways of the darker woman, who may now look better and is better turned out. Meanwhile the skinny little dark girl of yesteryear has learned makeup, filled out physically and turned out with a new inner confidence, spiced sometimes with an outer charm, gained over a lifetime of having to win friends in the face of her physical disadvantages, or settle with being whipped down and back in a corner like a flower up against the wall.

That's why — without meaning to knock the lightskinned sister — we black women secretly cheer when women like Barbara Jordan, Oprah Winfrey, Jackie-Joyner Kersee, Maya Angelou, Gladys Knight, and Patti LaBelle get over in the world carrying an inner beauty that helps to elevate the external definitions of the darker sister.

People still haven't understood why, when they drive through the poor communities, the women and kids tend to be of blacker hue than in "the Gold Coast." Historically, children and adults descending from white slavemasters got better breaks from whites and blacks. On top of that, black males choosing females might rescue a lightskinned woman from the meanest ghetto streets while the darker woman couldn't even get a job up front, say, as a receptionist or cashier. If too many black athletes now appear to think that a white woman goes with the scholarship, black M.D.'s and lawyers have long appeared to think that a lightskinned woman went with the Cadillac.

But, "my, how times have changed," sociologist Robert Staples (a neighbor of mine) once observed to me. "The black medical doctors are now driving a Mercedes Benz with a *white* wife sitting on the passenger's side — in some cases, both were trade-ins." The black sociologist further revealed that "some of the biggest protests against black men marrying white women come from lightskinned black women who were the biggest losers in this trading up for a 'better' model."

Many lightskinned women are even angrier when black men marry white women because they are the ones that have been displaced, who've been bumped off their throne. The black men who chose the white women were as brainwashed as we were, came on the slaveships as we did, and thought that, once they had gotten their education and made their mark, they needed what the white man has to be complete. After Jim Crow fell, many black professional males saw that they no longer needed to settle for the lightskinned black woman, the imitation white woman, but could go straight to the real thing.

The mulatto actress, Lonette McKee, who was the first black woman to play Julie in "Show Boat," was just one of the lightskinned sisters who complain of being too light to be cast in black roles and too "exotic" to play generic (white) ones. Her passionate speech in Spike Lee's "Jungle Fever" about being "too black for one world and too white for another" didn't fly too well with the many darker women who're too black for either world.

Hollywood has a history of resisting the idea of leading

romantic roles for black women, especially darker ones, who tend to be restricted to comedy and tragedy. Whoopi Goldberg, Cicely Tyson, Ethel Waters, Butterfly McQueen, come to mind. Sisters in the middle of the color spectrum are often prostitutes. But they'll paint a lightskinned Lonette McKee down a shade or two to play Zora Neale Hurston, never making up a darkskinned woman — even the most attractive by other Eurocentric guidelines — such as Phyllis Yvonne Stickney, to play a lightskinned Lena Horne.

If you notice the black female television news anchors, they don't tend to be particularly dark or African-featured nor light or "high-yellow." They're typically in-between, like copper-colored white mannequins, and soaps operas are worse, using mainly milk chocolate caramel black women. But you can bet that when there's a role for a villain or a prostitute, the dark woman will be cast. The recent rash of black dysfunctionals paraded as guests on daytime television talk shows also tend to be rather darkskinned and not too pretty by white accounts. When the white woman replaced the lightskinned woman, she pushed the darkskinned woman even farther down the totem pole.

So we needn't condemn ourselves, or one another — didn't start the color complex any more than the rift in black male/female relationships. But we must take part of the blame for perpetuating it.

Whoopi Goldberg is quick to correct an interviewer, who asks her about the difficulty of African-American women landing acceptable Hollywood roles, saying she's "not an African-American woman." "I'm not from Africa, I was born in America." Whoopi goes on to explain that she's an American culturally and otherwise, not African and that any problem she has is because she's a woman.

Today, young adult mulatto women, more than their male

counterparts, are beginning to call for a new racial category of mixed blacks in the United States. We may end up like Brazil, with a color caste topped by a light skinned elite, with the darker purer blacks pushed even farther down the hierarchy of beauty, as we degenerate into Black Anglo Saxonism.

Black Women Who Marry White Men

Few people are aware that at least half as many black women married white men as black men married white women during the past ten years. Some prefer trips to Europe over Africa because they hear that Italian men love black women. Some who know about this trend don't care that much about black women marrying white as they do when black men marry out of the race, mainly because it's a sleeper, a quiet and recent trend, not talked about in public and private discourse. But the bottom line is that we have a surplus of black women, not a shortage, as in the case of black men. Still, sisters should know, if they don't already, that a lot of brothers get extremely angry when they see a black woman with a white man.

When a black man is with a white woman, people often say that she has money (though sisters say you can look at her and tell she's one step away from "po white trash"). Or "she can open doors for 'em." "She can open doors for him, because white people will know he's on their side,' or, excepting a racist, will "like him for liking one of them — at least they can see he ain't a black nationalist."

Usually it's a black man, trying to justify his choice under fire, who says the white woman has all those advantages. Many are lucky to get a chance to drive her Wolkswagen. There're black women who've lucked into money too, but most black people who marry white are lucky to get somebody on their social class level. Rich people tend to marry rich people, and poor people marry poor people, whether they're white or black.

Even when the white person is richer, usually the sister is also rich, just marrying somebody richer. Maybe more important is the fact that they are famous, because white people — rich and poor — who marry black appear to go out mainly for high profile blacks.

On the other hand, black women call all the white women they see a brother with "white trash." But the same black woman who sees a black woman with a white man will say she has "a real catch," and she knows "he's got something." "I'll bet he treats her like a queen, puts her on a pedestal." She forgets this is the descendant and the colleague of the same men who've denied black women access to the pedestal. One source of this mythology is probably the number of white men who, when they marry black, appear to find the dark black woman exotic with African features, the same kind of woman most likely to be shunned by black men. To the extent that dark women are shunned and perhaps misued by black men, the notion will be fed that white men treat all black women they marry better. Indeed, all women. "Honey, he treats her just like she's Miss Anne."

This is something black men and women do — exaggerate the good qualities of white people while diminishing the quality of their own. There's something more going on here than the simple maxim that "the grass is greener on the other side of the fence." To begin with, all groups think the other side is better. You'll hear white women say it's a myth that white men treat them better than black men treat white women.

However, when the races cross, they bring with them the stranger effect; that is, people are more polite and conciliatory to strangers than to people with whom they're familiar, more likely to put on their best manners when they greet them at the door than they would if they know it's just Jake, and less likely to argue with strangers over little things. If you wanted to, you could sit in a restaurant or public place and tell which couples are married, or how intimate they are, by the way they carry on a conversation. If they're polite and formal, they probably aren't lovers or intimates or are just getting started. But if they're discourteous and openly hostile, they're probably married, certainly intimately connected, if they're together.

But I've found when I do seminars that black women had very deep concerns on a personal level and a societal level about being with white men, Asians, Hispanics, anything other than a black man. The strange thing about this is if the women were not famous, they get accusations from the other sisters that they must have married white because they couldn't find a black man.

The black woman herself, about to marry white, will frequently say, if our men are thought to be sexually superior to the men of other races, why am I relegated to going out of this race to something inferior? The idea of marrying a white man also brings up historical overtones to a black woman, that many of their grandfathers, their ancestors, were dangled from trees by the same breed of men that now proposes to share their bed. They also believed that people see them as somehow primitive, exotic and animalistic, even if the white mate doesn't.

There was this black woman who, prior to marrying white, used to get with me and a few other sisters and gossip about the goings-on in our society, especially on black male/female relationship. They used to hate the fact when it was time to go to an all-white party, because they knew that, even if it was in the dead of winter, all the shades would be wide open, you didn't know who was looking at you. The black culture is to shut your shades down. We've lived in greater peril, from Klansmen and white night riders in the old South to drivebys in the inner city. She talked about how, at white parties, you had to stand for hours holding cocktail glasses, shifting from one leg to the other, making smalltalk ("how do you know Heather?"). When the food is finally served, it is frequently replete with cheeses, cheese sauces, or wine and cheese (clearly not a black party, because of the low black tolerance for lactose in dairy products). In the course of the party, people eat from each other's plate, sampling this and sampling that, while black people tend to be "persnickety," they rarely eat from one another's plate.

A few months later, this same woman married a white man. When I went to one of her early dinner parties, I got to her house and what did I see, from our nationalist friend who had laughed so hard with me sometimes she'd fall to the floor holding her stomach when we would talk about the differences in the black and white parties. I stepped in there and saw a room filled with whites, doing just as we'd said, shifting from leg to leg, Mozart playing drearily in the background, with wine and cheese, shades so wide you could see the moon and the stars, the same things we'd talked about. The sister not only married a nondescript white individual but took on the bland aspects of white culture. Where she once had Lionel Richie, James Brown, Ray Charles, Anita Baker, Aretha Franklin (the likes of Mariah Carey and Whitney Houston were "too white" for this sister), she now had CD's of Bon Jovi, Guns 'n Roses, Grace Jones, and Rick Springsteen (Tom Jones, Elvis Presley, Vanilla Ice, were now "too ethnic" for her).

Still, a lot of black women have concluded that, if they have to deal with anything other than a black man, they would rather do without, because they can't erase the historical and social baggage and paraphernalia of black and white sex on the slave plantation and in the Antebellum period and the South during Reconstruction and Jim Crow segregation.

Almost without exception, all of these black women who're

off into relationships with white men say that it's the white culture or the culture of whatever person they marry, not the black culture, that tends to prevail. That certainly appears to be true in cases where black men marry white women.

The Brother Who Marries White

You've been around this brother and heard him huffing and puffing about "a woman is a woman to me, we're all one, skin color don't matter." Does it or doesn't it? Wonder why he spends most of his time with you-know-who? Wonder why he screams racism at the drop of a hat, or the drop of the white man's hammer on his coconut head (brown on the outside, white on the inside, water on the brain)?

Quite often, "Blood" is married to a white woman but can constantly be found railing and crying the holy blues about "the white man." Usually he can give you a three-hour diatribe aiming to prove there're no differences between white and black women. But from the moment you first heard him say that on a sexual romantic basis there was no difference between the white woman and the black woman, you knew right away that you were in direct competition with the white woman, that this brother had a hangup on whatever differences he thinks he sees in white women while claiming he does not. I mean these brothers can find a white woman in the dark. Some of the floosies they come up with — obviously just because they're white — can look like they just came out of a cave, because the brother was "sho nuf" dealing in the dark. Heard one fellow say it's okay if she's obese, it just gives him more white to love.

The only thing that matters to this brother is her color. He may be off at the drop of a handkerchief from any woman, but if she's white she doesn't have to drop her handkerchief. All she has to do is be — white. He might fool with a sister a little bitty while, but the first thing you know he's skipping right on back to Anne.

So, if this brother isn't for you, young sister, run now, as fast and as far as you can. At least look at this brother with one eye open, or give him a quick course in Consciousness 101A, because he's going to have to be enlightened (or endarkened) real quick. But the danger here is, as soon as he learns a little consciousness, a little blackness, he's liable to take a notion to be a leader — with the white woman by his side, coaching him behind the scenes and sometimes coming out front to the embarrassment of us all.

Heard a comedian say the other night that it's one thing for the brother to bring his white woman out to the black cultural affairs, even to seat her down front, but you just can't let her get up at the dance. One of them jumped up and joined the group doing the "electric slide" and messed up the whole line — the one time that black people get it together on whether to go left of right is when they're doing the electric slide.

So, be careful if you decide to stick around this brother. It may be hard to keep from internalizing some of the things he's putting down. You have to understand he has the media, story book, TV and films behind his game as well as subtle reinforcements from four hundred years of the most complete and cunning brainwashing yet known to recorded history. You can get to wondering and, before you know it, you start agreeing with him that, "all women do have breasts, all women do have hips and legs, all women do or should get pap smears, just like all men have, or once had testicles. So it doesn't matter if brothers prefer blondes."

Some of the details of this brother's song may well be true but things could only work like that in an ideal society, a raceless society where race plays no part. If race wasn't a factor, we wouldn't even be dealing with this subject now. But it is.

Quiet as it's kept, there're a whole lot of sisters marrying out now to white boys. But let's face it, just between you and me, some of the sisters who marry out couldn't find a black man. With the exception of the variety of sisters who'd spend their last dime to be white (Whoopi Goldberg, Diana Ross, the late Pearl Bailey, come to mind), the overwhelming majority of black women who marry white do so because there were no eligible black men left to them. (Of course some brothers will now tell you they couldn't find an eligible sister, but you know that's a lie). We know there's no shortage of black women.

I've interviewed some of the surplus sisters for this book. They said such things as they married a white man only because they wanted babies and married to beat the biological clock. It was a matter of "What am I going to do?" But that doesn't stop some sisters from cocking their heads to the side and strolling down the street with the white boy like she's accomplished something.

In my motivational seminars, many speak of remembering the tales of white men raping defenseless black women in slavery time, and later in the Deep South, so they can't easily blot out memories of the predatory nature of the white man the way black men develop amnesia of the white woman's collaboration with the white man.

It's partly a thing about female sexuality, involving a lot of little subtleties and complications men don't care about. But it's also about the difference in the way black men and women experienced slavery. It's true that black men had to face humiliation, unable to free themselves or protect their women and children, or themselves from the lyncher's rope. They also had to work hard in the sun for nothing, but they weren't sexually violated every day the way black women were.

Missing the protection of her man, flat of her back with nobody to defend her and unable to defend herself while being compelled to submit to the nauseous cravings of the white slavemaster, sometimes while the white slavemistress looked on or turned her head or pretended she didn't see her man's degradation and his vile lust for the black slave woman's body. Talk about sexual harassment in the workplace; don't forget to include four centuries of sexual harassment of black women in the reparations package. After all the Japanese were recently forced to apologize to Korean women they forced into prositution when they invaded Korea.

For whatever reason, when it comes to marriageable black males, the stark reality is we have a very limited and dwindling supply. Problem is the white woman has a male shortage too. Not as harsh as ours, especially at the top, but enough to leave a horde of white women free to come over and try to rip-off already scarce black males. Worse, as I said before, the white woman wants the cream of the crop, she wants to marry up. For instance (as our figures at The Black Think Tank show), even when the white woman isn't a college person, she tends to marry a college black male. The black man gives her, trades off, his social status while she gives him her whiteness. She is the one who can validate his deepseated wish to be white, As Frantz Fanon (who was married to a white woman) pointed out in *Black Skin, White Mask,* if the coconut brother can be loved by the white woman who is loved by the white man, then he is white like the white man, he is a full human being — in his own twisted and pathological mind, he *is* white.

You know how we sisters, in our den sessions and private living room settings, like to talk about how the "successful" black man seems too ready to bolt from the black woman's nest into a sexual-romantic bond with the white woman. Looks like sometimes as soon as the brother gets a check or two above the welfare line, he alters his speech and starts his "climb" up the corporate ladder right into the arms of Miss Ann (Ms. Anne).

A few years ago, I was a guest expert on the Sally Jesse Raphael Show dealing with the subject, "Black Women Whose Husbands Left Them for White Women." Sally had a panel of black sisters who'd had that experience. The sisters were mad and they were tough. In any case, the producers ran the show over and over several times during the ratings sweeps. It happened that the television audience was almost all-white, except for a couple of sisters like the ones you always see pop up to take the side of the white point of view, trying to outwhite the whites.

I found myself on the same side with the panel, so we cooked a while. I revealed my survey of the black males who make up the more than 200,000 brothers who've married across the river. Some said they took up with white women as a way of "getting back at the white man." Some claimed black women are "too uptight" and don't want to engage in kinky sex, preferring to stick to the "missionary position." Others said the black woman "demands too many things." She wants him to work, to help around the house, to contribute to the family income beyond his capabilities and even to take night classes, while a white woman will let them "be" and will give him money on the side and let him drive her Volkswagen.

Funny how when you actually see a brother with a white woman and a Volkswagen she's standing there holding her purse while the brother has her blonde child by her first marriage on his back, drooling on his shoulder, with the diaper hanging around his neck. He's got two bags of groceries in his arms and using one foot to open the car door for her. This is the same brother who wouldn't do a thing for his first (black) wife. He didn't have time to help with the dishes. Washing the dishes was a threat to his manhood.

But he loses his mind when he gets with Anne. He becomes quickly acculturated, bringing her flowers, kissing cats, feigning an ear for classical music, giving her compliments, it's "so and so, dear," and "dear" this and "dear" that, "isn't that lovely" — all in a soap opera tone of voice, the same one who cursed and argued and called his black woman bitches all day and half the night. But with Anne, he acts like he thinks he's in heaven with an angel birth certificate.

Brother, fool, even if you don't care how white women gloat and laugh at your alleged frenzy for her freckled butt, do you understand the need of the black female for the black male? Do you understand that the black woman, in most cases, gave birth to you? Have you forgotten who raised you, Negro? Who cleaned your funky rear end, washed your dirty diapers and scuffled and scraped and saved so you could be ready when you grow up to amount to something and give back to the community and do your do? Why do you keep on bringing shame on yourself and our people and pain to black women and black children by your whey-eyed lolling after somebody other than your own? And then have the nerve sometimes to try to come back home. Sisters, we're going to have to take matters into our own hands and put a screeching stop to this splickety-split. We're going to have to stop letting these brothers crawl back into the black community and our empty nests after Anne gets through with his so-and-so and kicks his broke self out.

Start with giving the brother a litmus test, a romantic litmus test. That's what we've got to do. It isn't a surefire thing, but it provides a range or set of questions you can use for screening purposes. Let him flunk a question or two, but if he comes up short on too many, maybe you ought to beware, at least be aware.

What are some of the telltale signs of a coconut brother whose mind, whose heart, is white? First off, as we have said, he doesn't think there's any difference between black and white women, ask the brother who his heroes are. Have him tell you something about his past girlfriends. Find out where he grew up and went to school. If he spent all the days of his youth with white boys and girls, he may have lost his blackness and his appreciation for blackness and all things black. He may not even be able to tolerate listening to black ("gut bucket") music for more than a minute or two, but is often heavy into hillbilly (Elvis, Willie Nelson) music or a pretense of being enraptured by the classics, may even use Beethoven or Bach as background to the Shakespeare he likes to read you on a moonlit night. A lot of times he's forgotten how to talk black, can't get with hanging with black males anymore, but spends all his time with Burt and Bard. He doesn't like rhythm and may be turned all the way off from soul. Sister, leave this brother alone.

Not that it's necessarily all his fault. Maybe he's spent all of his life in a certain milieu, as he often says, "I was the only black in my class" or "I was the only black on my block" and "I was the only black this and that..." Maybe you'd better check out his weekend activities also, his favorite haunts, coffee shops, his best male friends. If he's hanging with the white boys; he may be panting after their sisters.

I mean, if you're going to protect yourself from a coconut lover, you've got to watch what he loves and has loved romantically and platonically and otherwise. For instance, Bryant Gumbel has a black wife (as of this writing, at least), but you know if the brother ever gets another whack at it, a black woman might not have an even break.

A brother may be interested in you now, but that doesn't

mean he's not still hopping behind the white woman. Better check him out now. Look at Sugar Ray Leonard, who had been with his black wife, his first wife, since adolescence. Remember when he fought in the Olympics in Montreal with her picture in a locket around his ankle? As soon as they broke up, the brother headed for his first inclination. There's been some hint she might not be white, but she looks white and certainly is white minded — every last one of her bridesmaids were clearly white, so you be the judge.

So if you want to save yourself a lot of trouble, a litmus test is as important to you as an SAT test is to a college registrar, if not more so. As a matter of fact, you might get together your own litmus test in other areas of his mindset besides this love or potential love of the white woman. For instance, whether he's a committed type of person in an overall sense, because as we said before, statistics and proximity, if nothing else, make him more likely to leave you for another sister than for a white woman. Will the brother work? Can you get along? Do you have any common interests, likes or dislikes? Does he want anything out of life at all? Do you like the same kind of people? These are some of the questions you could use to check your BMW out real good, before you get in high gear and head down the wrong highway on a "rainbow" driven roller coaster ride.

Watch out for the celebrity lover, with too much popularity. Maybe you should even watch celebrities per se who would be your lover. If you aspire to a celebrity life, you should have started working your strategy in college, if not in high school, because by the time they get to college, many of those most likely to become celebrities, the young athletes, appear to think that a white woman goes with the scholarship. Both of baseball's MVP's (of the American League and the National League for 1993) were married to white women as pictured back-to-back or butt-to-butt in the news media.

Sexual Jungle Fever — The Age of the Crossover. Without trying to exhaust any total list, let me give you a peep at some of the most recent MVP's from the entire athletic world. Speaking of "Jungle Fever," there's now athletic jungle fever, political jungle fever, jungle fever here, jungle fever there, and jungle fever just about everywhere. In baseball there's Barry Bonds, the San Francisco Giant slugger, last year's National League MVP and the only baseball player in history to win the MVP three years in a row, Bonds is married to white Sun Bonds, though they're momentarily going through a divorce. Which one will his next bond be with?

Remember former baseball star Reggie Jackson's repeat performances with the bleached blonde apples of his eye? Not to mention Quincy Jone's threepeats. The Chicago white Sox's Frank Thomas, (the American League's Most Valuable Player) is married to white Miss Elise. Sugar Ray Leonard is married to a lady who could pass for a mulatto but in any case had an all-white female court in her wedding ceremony as pictured in *Jet,* revealing where her head is and undoubtedly the secret to the ambiguity of her lineage.

So if you want an MVP, it might be a good idea to enroll at a black college in a small country town, a place like Itta Bena, Mississippi, where the wife of Jerry Rice, the 49ers all-time record-breaking super wide receiver of the 49ers, apparently saw something special in a skinny young brother who had grown up catching bricks for his bricklaying father. Or like, Jesse Jackson's wife, Jackie, who hooked up with a brother whose lisp couldn't stop him from hugging the podium at Greensboro's North Carolina A & T College.

You can't sit around hanging back waiting until these brothers enter the rainbow coalition, sister. When television A Team's Mr. T attended Prairie View College before getting tossed out for leading a campus rebellion, he went largely unnoticed or was seen as "crazy" until he came to fame in a "Rocky" film. Then everybody started slipping him notes ard calling him for dinner. Mr. T told male and female alike not to bother to call him "for no dinner," that if you didn't recognize his worth when he was on the streets, "you just messed up" and missed out on a good thing. Don't even try to bring a losers ticket to the winners gate.

Check the brothers out *before* they crossover. Learn to recognize a brother's worth and potential before the white woman does. To tell the truth though, many sisters now are guilty of the crossover themselves — quiet as it is kept. Diana Ross has gone to the well with a white man twice in a row, after her love hangover with Barry Gordy. Sugar Ray Robinson' ex-wife, crossed over the line as soon as she broke up with the only black man she ever loved. Even Muhammad Ali's ex, Khalilah was pictured in the trades and tabloids with what "sho nough" looked like a white Arab fiance. Alice Walker is floundering between expressing her love for trees, from her hilltop California mansion after a lengthy marriage to a white man. According to *Ms* magazine, she eventually got around to living and loving a brother who looks white, and also was married to a white woman before her. So apparently his hookup with Alice Walker was the closest either one of them could come to loving anybody black. Carol Mosely Braun, the only black member of the U.S. Senate, can now say she's hooked up with an Ivy League trained African from the continent, but Mr. Braun was white. For that matter, the only other black U.S. Senator since Reconstruction, Ed Brooke, was married to a white woman. That's one hundred per cent white for black U.S. senators y'all, Lord, Jesus.

The Crossover Imperative has been fueled also by the rise of rainbow politics. Hillary Clinton's friend and mentor, Marian Wright Edelman, is married to Mr. Edelman. Julian Bond, after a long marriage to a member of Atlanta, Georgia's second or third generation black social elite, has now picked up a homely white woman. Clarence Thomas sat unflinchingly holding on to his white wife's hand during the dramatic Senate confirmation hearing carried live on national network television as he fought to become the second black man in history to serve on the U.S. Supreme Court. Vernon Jordan, who once headed the National Urban League and is now a high-stakes black consultant to Clinton, is married to a white woman, now that his late wheelchair-bound black wife, who suffered from crippling multiple sclerosis, is gone.

When President Clinton came to office and put on his high-level economic conference in Little Rock, I noted that at least five of the visible black individuals in a *New York Times* partial listing of 40 persons invited, included: Spellman president Johnetta Cole (once married for many years to a white man); sociologist William Wilson, author of *The Declining Significance of Race,* written while reclining with his white wife. (Wilson, like Marian Wright Edelman, has received the MacArthur Foundation's lucrative ''genius'' award, which repeatedly has appeared to favor integrationist and the service of integrationism with a relentless and unadulterated singularity of purpose.)

As a matter of fact, the brothers and sisters invited to the Bill Clinton *economic* summit were most distinguished, if anything, by the fact that none was an economist or business leader and, though they had won high appointments and acclaim in white and white-backed organizations, none has ever made any money on their own, though some are specialists in interpreting or administering to ''the Black underclass'' at the salaried or funded behest of white mainstream corporate powers-that-be.

Welcome, young sister, to the Age of the Crossover in black history. The crossover era first entered the scene and got its name in the field of pop music when white people such as Linda Ronstadt and Tom Jones launched the crossover music wave to follow in the earnest footsteps and example so brilliantly etched by Elvis Pressley, the Beatles and the Rolling Stones, exploiting and imitating black music and black singing and dancing styles.

Soon black people started trying to croon like white people, just about to yodel. With the exception of the ambiguous musical form called "rap," interjected by inner city youth, the result is the virtual desertion of rhythm and blues, as we once knew it, till now we have the sometimes pitiful, soulless arhythmic white renditions while black singers try to sing like white people trying to sing like black people trying to sing like white people.

The turning point to the Crossover Imperative — reflected in a creeping silent doubling of white-black marriages in the single decade of the slumbering 1970s on the heels of the passing of the brief, four-year late 1960s "Black-power-black-is-beautiful" awakening — was perhaps best concealed in the much-heralded late 1970s television mini-series, *Roots*.

The cast of *Roots* was conspicuous in the number of leading players who were or had been married white: for example, Ben Vereen, Louis Gossett, O.J. Simpson, Maya Angelou, Richard Roundtree, and Leslie Uggams. Despite its focus on the story of the kidnapping of blacks from Africa into chattel slavery in America, *Roots* may inadvertently have told us more about the future than the past and might well have been entitled. *The Return of the Black Anglo Saxons.*

Ask any black man who shows a certain passion for white women why he has this white woman Jones or why he sings his sorry blues for Snow White, and chances are he'll name "forbidden fruit," euphemism for what one of the most prominent black female politicians in this country calls "the pink pussy syndrome."

Black psychiatrist Frantz Fanon, who married a white woman while living and working in Algiers, concluded in his first book, *Black Skin, White Mask* that, based on his clinical observations, it isn't possible for a member of an oppressed group, while still living under a situation of oppression. Fanon went so far as to to say that the very wish to sleep with a white woman is essentially a desire to be white. The black male so constituted wants to be validated as white, Fanon explains, and "who but the white woman can do this for him?"

This is why it seems to matter so little what the white woman looks like. Sometime you'll hear a sister say, "I can't get over this; you can look at this brother and see he's in a doublebreasted jacket and can still button it over his stomach, so you know he wouldn't be fooling with no sister who looks like this white woman." Especially if she's big and fat. But when a white woman is fat, it seems some brothers feels it's just more white for them to love. You know how sometimes you can see a real pretty brother with the ugliest white frumpet. (And when she chooses to marry a black man, she wants the cream of the crop, including the college-educated black male, even when she herself is not a college person). The brother gives her his social status, his social potency, and she gives him her whiteness. You recognize the result of this today as "jungle fever."

Where Have You Gone

Where have you gone
with your confident
walk with
your crooked smile

why did you leave
me
when you took your
laughter
and departed

are you aware that
with you
went the sun
all light
and what few stars
there were?

where have you gone
with your confident
walk your
crooked smile the
rent money
in one pocket and
my heart
in another. . . .

© *Mari Evans*
Indianapolis, Indiana

The Eurocentric Brother

Eurocentric brothers can usually be found somewhere in the ivory towers, very integrated places, though they are not unknown in the ebony towers. They generally consider themselves as the "cream of the crop." Others call them, "bourgies", a "tom," an "oreo," a "Black Anglo Saxon" or simply a "coconut," (brown on the outside, white on the inside, with a fair amount of water on the brain).

But, if it's social potency or social position you're looking for, you may be on the right trail when you travel among this pompous populace. They include affirmative action officers, assistant deans, provosts, multi-cultural coordinators, special assistants to the vice president in charge of internal affairs and the entire gamut of what used to be called HNIC (Head Nigger in Charge) or Special Assistant to the Assistant to whatnot. There're also HNOCs (Head Niggers on Campus).

The coconut brother can be found in any gathering of ethnic studies directors and black studies coordinators, especially when they have dual assignments to sociology or humanities departments (or departments of their generic field) so that they can claim to be in the "Government Department" or whatever department and skip back and forth between unholy endeavors to be socially acceptable here and politically correct there, going for integration with an Afrocentric flair.

The coconut or Eurocentric brother is the one you see sitting against the wall in a simulated yoga posture with his shoes off wriggling his toes amid the we're-all-one atmosphere of a white party, or the one waltzing around pinching the stem of his cocktail glass and asking everybody he meets "And what do *you* do?"

If this is your cup of tea — make that high tea, with cream and crumpets — you're going to have to get ready for a tactile highbrow performance.

If the Eurocentric brother is working in academe, the more prestigious the university the more he's probably been handpicked to pass the *whiteness litmus test*. I mean these brothers are usually thoroughly tried and true, checked, crosschecked, over a lifetime of tomming through foolproof white referral systems and job interview screenings. He can cock his head for hours and tell you about all of the grants he's received from the white mainstream foundations or the government to uplift and raise the consciousness of blacks (pronounced "b--lacks".) There isn't a black mark on this brother anywhere except his birthmark.

When he's away from the campus, he identifies himself as working in "the dominant culture." If he works for a black university, it's always "historically black" only in concession to the handful of nearby white farm youth who sometimes enroll in a black college from time to time to pick up a convenient diploma and run back to their white communities by night.

But again, if it's economic security you want, this may be your man. He's a master at white chitchat and careful to keep himself safe from any alienation of the white powers that be.

When a controversy broke out at San Francisco State University, involving the painting of religious symbols which some students associated with bigotry on a mural of Malcolm X, a Eurocentric brother in charge of a sizable "Afrocentric" grant reportedly said that he couldn't risk his grant money to speak out on "these kinds" of issues. Another brother who claimed to be an authority on African-American art and culture could not be located to make any public statement.

Even the Afrocentric nationalists on campus, while draped down to the ground in African attire and cultural commentary, preferred to meet with the students by night or by telephone to avoid being seen with them. Many Eurocentric brothers will talk a great game of "revolutionary struggle" on the telephone, in the corridors, in the airports where they can stand and take the floor, but when you're looking for somebody to talk to beyond the choir, they can't be found. An attorney in the Los Angeles area, prominent in the black Egyptology movement, confides that he recently sought and received permission from a leading national talk show to amass some black intellectuals prominent in the "melanin" movement (the idea that the melanin of the skin, which gives it the black color, imbibes blacks with a number of superior qualities). The attorney couldn't get any of the melanin experts to come on the show and tell white folks what they'd been telling black folks at melanin conferences and Afrocentric this and that since the end of the 1960s.

Most Eurocentrics don't even claim to be blackminded. Not that some of them aren't radical or "progressive" or committed to the cause of social change. It's just that they "can't see color," they "just see people." "It isn't about race, it's about people; we're all niggers," they giggle in knowing delight. They are fond of calling everybody from white liberals, gays and "womyn" to hillbillies and Allegheny Mountain coal miners "the new niggers." They are forever referring to "women, minorities and the poor," always in that order, and they can espouse lofty theories of integration and diversity and classical white feminism sufficient to win the hearts of Gloria Allred and Bill Clinton.

More radical Eurocentrics include "rainbow" blacks who see everything in terms of class or "ecology." So you're going to have to know all about the history of Marx and Engels, if not Lenin and Hegel. You'll have plenty of time because, in most instances, you're going to have to wait until this brother has had his fill of Ms. Anne.

While you're at it, ask yourself if you want to live in a university community in a small town near Mo Betta, Montana where you're usually the first and, sometimes, the last black woman ever to arrive in those parts. If so, you should get to work honing your ability to live two lives, the one you present to his white colleagues and the one you must return to when you're visiting back home in Arkansas or attending the Afrocentric convention in Jackson, Mississippi.

Aside from listening carefully to their conversation and scrutinizing their leanings and loyalties closely, there are other ways to screen out the Eurocentric, if you so desire. To begin with, beware of the clean shaven brother. Chances are, instead of a black man, you'll be getting a "white boy." This is especially true in the age of the crossover imperative for black men who wish to move up in the white world, in the epoch of the rainbow coalition and rainbow consciousness.

Because black people tend to look up to anybody heralded in the mass media, any successful black person, especially those who occasionally speak out on racial issues with a militant-sounding voice — unless they come to represent some concrete affront to the race — many black persons who are closer to whites in their loyalties and the way they think become heroes to blacks. Anybody smiled on by the media and the powers that be become our leaders, whether they are reading poetry at a presidential inauguration or distinguished professors of black studies at Harvard or whatever conspicuous success in the white world. Many people, by contrast, will be wholly unaware of the obstacles a black perspective presents to black individuals who would move up the white-dominated corporate ladder.

Books have been written about blacks in corporate life complaining of the way they have to leave their blackness outside the corporate door — don't even talk about blackness or being black while you're at work. Some brothers and sisters feel they literally have to become "bi-lingual," adopting "proper" or "white airs" at work but resuming a black dialect or "street" brogue by night or in relaxed conversation with non-corporate blacks. This combines with the particular white fear and antipathy for the black male to require that socially mobile black males take special pains to let white supervisors know that they're no threat. The result is the Eurocentric brother.

Add to this the fact that the black male is blocked from the avenues to social potency (wealth, position, power and prestige), leaving them inclined to overcompensate in the physical, including the athletic and the sexual, or activities focused on proficiency in deployment of the physical body. Even the underclass black male is likely to pay particular attention to how he sits, with a clear element of machismo, the way he walks — usually with an ultra-masculine saunter or strut, when so much as going down the street. For the black male, facial hair, (mustache or a beard or both) can comprise the most conspicuous components of his masculinity.

By contrast, the black male who would make it in the corporate world tends to find it advantageous to be close-cropped or clean-shaven; hence the emergence of a social type of black male we might call The Clean-shaven Brother. The clean-shaven brother is not to be confused with the baldheaded brother discussed elsewhere

52

in this book. But, because of the close association of hair and masculinity in the culture of the ghetto, when a brother is involuntarily bald, he is inclined to cultivate a conspicuous and copious beard as compensation.

A colleague has noted that voluntarily baldheaded brothers tend to be anal-retentive, preoccupied with orderliness, stinginess, obstinacy and an excessive need for control of others in the service of the self. She points to similarities in the personalities of actor Lou Gossett, Mr. T., musician Issac Hayes, television show host Montel Williams (who once did an entire show on men with shining domes), not to mention a number of prominent black nationalist intellectuals. Keep your eyes peeled for the peeled-headed-brother.

I should warn you that a lot of sisters with experience dating hairless brothers have proclaimed that there is a certain amount of narcissism that goes with the territory. If the narcissist is an individual who, having given up on the hope of being loved by others, focuses on loving himself, this may be why these brothers have tended to rationalize their baldness or sublimate it in a belief that women see their peeled heads as gnome-like symbols of terrestrial patriarchy, as gargantuan phallic symbols. While these brothers aren't as slick as they appear or pretend to be, they frequently may be seen walking into the middle of a hushed room consumed with the false impression that all the women present are sexually harboring unbridled hopes and imaginations upon their shining cerebral knobs.

Not that a lot of them don't have presence compared to the brothers who carefully brush the one or two strands left back across their head in the mistaken belief that they are clever in the art of concealment, like the tall woman who slumps into a room with shoulders drooped instead of walking right in with her shoulders unequivocally erect and emblematic of her showstopping stature.

53

If you, yourself are inclined to stop a show, in fact, you may want to dip into the pool of baldheaded brothers. Many, maybe in compensation, are high-achievers, assertive and aggressive. The trouble is, it too often goes to their head.

There's a baldheaded brother I know in Nashville who likes to tell ladies up front: "if you have no hair in front, you're a thinker; if you have no hair in back, you're a lover. But if you have no hair in the front or the back, you think you're a lover when it's all in the mind."

The Afrocentric Brother

If the Afrocentric nationalist is your ideal BMW, you've got to be ready to be a great listener, perhaps a bit of a dreamer, or some kind of romantic idealist. Unlike the nationalistic activists of the 1960s, high-tech nationalists of today are do-nothing nationalists and mainly just talk and talk and talk about white supremacy and the glories of ancient African civilization before the coming of the white man. Mostly their militancy is verbal, symbolic and ceremonial. Instead of confronting the system of oppression, they rationalize, justify, and make apologies for the black male's demise and, often as not, the bullheaded obstinance of white domination.

Typically employed by some white institution, and seeking ways to move up within its hierarchy in some way, they may harp relentlessly against the established order during informal gatherings in the sanctity of somebody's living room or parlor: "the man's got his foot on my back." "Looks like the black woman thinks I ought to have as much as the man." Though he customarily wears Pan-African attire costumed to exceed his commitment, as soon as somebody prosposes a plan of action for black uplift, he darts for the door, scrambles for the history books, or hops a plane to the Pyramids on the continent of Africa, or somewhere in the Diaspora.

I mean this brother can boast all day long of knowing the names of every African king in 400 B.C. or of sailing on the Nile, and he's forever fashioning some African ceremony or ritual. He may even take trips to Las Vegas to stay in its Luxor Egyptian Hotel, with its simulation Nile river and touristic Egyptian replicas, including the likes of Sphinx sandwiches, Hatshepsut hamburgers, Dynasty hot dogs, Pyramid pickles, Kushite coffee, camel cakes, Nefertari nibbles, and assorted Imhotep edibles.

Let me say that, as I see it, there are two categories of Afro nationalists — the formally educated and the informally educated. Here we're talking of course about the formally educated, the degreed nationalist, who works frequently at or around a university and its community, where his African attire is more socially acceptable and can be employed to pump him up in his militant posturing strategy to hide his aversion for activism. Unsuspecting students frequently are persuaded to equate and measure his militancy by the amount of mud cloth and kinte he owns. This brother believes that black males in suits and ties (who in fact in some cases may be doing more to change black conditions for the better than he is) can't be anything but "bourgies" (pretentious members or would-be members of the black bourgeoisie). At the same time, it allows him to exploit the suspect militancy of mass media-made black intellectuals such as Shelby Steele and Cornel West. Manytimes the high-tech Afronationalist will condemn the Shelby Steeles, the Cornel Wests or some other well-hyped Eurocentric nationalist while snuggling up to them anytime they come to town.

As for the informally educated or homemade nationalist, his problem and his persona are usually proscribed by his "self-employment" or his hustle if he can't dignify it as employment, because his penchant for wearing dreads and kinte cloth in the office cloaks him in a cocoon of resistance and, in any case, is not likely to sit well with white employers or supervisors.

This brother delights in haranguing white colleagues and coworkers at coffee breaks about how "we built the Pyramids." With white feminists, he falls back on the undocumented notion that "we had matriarchies" in Ancient Africa and Egypt, as opposed to understanding and doing something about why we live today in a broken patriarchy.

Not that many of these brothers aren't, or can't be, great catches. But, if you're into finery and material things, gifts, birthdays, holiday excursions, trips and cruises to exotic places, you may need to scan another category of brothers for your BMW. The Afronationalist brother may be quick enough to accept a gift from you. But, if and when you expect the same in return, he'll likely tell you that is "bourgeoisie."

I once met a 26-year old female buppy (black upwardly mobile urban professional) who complained of having shopped for days for just the right Christmas "toys" (cashmere coat, VCR, Genesis games, etc.) for her Afrocentric lover. I mean this sister had spent many hours in the finest stores looking for gifts for the brother, and he knew she had. When the big morning, Christmas morning came, he was over to her apartment early as expected. When he came in, she had the Charles Brown classic, "Merry Christmas Baby" on the stereo. The brother sat down and chimed in with Charles Brown on such phrases as, "I haven't had a drink this morning, but I'm all lit up like a Christmas tree," pausing just long enough to refill his cup of latte.

She opened her gifts for him — which were many — amid gushes of gratitude from him, (Aw-w, Baby, you shouldn't have done this), then looked for hers. He said, "Oh, I don't believe in material things," and went on and on about how Christmas had become too commercial," how "black people spend eleven months trying to payoff debts from December," that, anyway, he was a follower of the new black African-oriented Kwanzaa.

So the sister decided to take everything in stride — why not? — and wait for Kwanzaa, which started the next day and actually involves giving gifts and fruits every day for seven days in a row. Needless to say, as Kwanzaa came and went, she discovered that he loved everything about Kwanzaa, *except* the idea of gifts and gift-giving. He wanted to know "why we couldn't just give of ourselves."

After collecting her gifts back (or those she could find the receipts for), she decided to look elsewhere for a BMW who wanted to share more than "spirituality."

It may be that, regardless of a brother's ideology, when you discover that your BMW is merely a Black Man Wanting, then is the time to do the converse of the Booker T. strategy of dropping your buckets where you are. Pick up your bucket and run. Head for clearer waters, uncontaminated by superficial belief systems and difficult dichotomies, before it's too late to avoid a mindset filled with bitterness and wasted time, unrequited wishes and unpaid regrets that will clutter your relationship or become the unchecked and invisible baggage that you carry or drag from one relationship to another.

The Bisexual Brother

We've all had a friend or known someone who finally found the perfect man — a prince charming, a BMW, just too good to be true. Then, low and behold, after a beautiful wedding in splendor suitable for any black royalty, that took everything you'd saved up (practically putting your grandmother out of house and home), when the honeymoon to Nassau or Hawaii is over, the love lights may go down low as you discover your BMW is a cross dipper, a switch hitter tipping through the tall tulips, loving both women and men.

It wasn't exactly something you heard. There was simply no denying it once you walked in and caught him in a compromising position, in bed with his buddy Jack that afternoon. "I had no idea he was that way," you tell your friends, but many say behind your back that it was nothing but denial.

Did your friends know it before you did? Didn't you see him with all his — shall we say "delicate" friends? Didn't you wonder why he started to lose interest in you sexually, when you hadn't lost your shape? How could you know the signs of a savvy switch hitter? Just because he no longer noticed your Teddies (straight out of Victoria's Secret), or was watching his weight more than you were watching yours? Just because his form-fitting jeans, cutting into his narrow hips, were tighter than yours? What could you make of the fact that the business meeting, or the lodge, or the fraternity meetings, started to extend through the weekend? That all of a sudden your he-man-get-down-in-the-struggle warrior is wearing more earrings than you, in pierced ears to boot?

When you met your BMW, he already possessed a certain gentility, but he was eligible and loved to have a good time. And it was a good time; good wine, good music, regular dining to candle light in the best of restaurants, He was so gregarious, so acceptable to your family. He was even a smash hit with your friends. Everybody loved your superman, so why not you? He could show his cultivated masculine courtesy to the women and command unquestioning respect from the men who came under the spell of his cleverly feigned masculine poise. And everybody, I mean everybody, loved his genial, caring ways, coupled with an incomparable sense of duty and responsibility, a gentleman par excellence.

I mean this man always knew just the right clothing for you to wear. He knew the matching colors, what was flattering to your skin and your color, your figure and your face, what would make you stand out. The brother was avant garde; knew the colors that were coming down the pike miles and miles before they got to the stores. He had an intuitive sense of what the new designs would be. This is the very reason women in the public eye, first ladies of entertainment, first ladies of politics, first ladies of the evening, women who want to make special fashion statements will so often have gay male friends to tell them what to wear. You've seen the large number of gays in the world of haute coutour. The icon of fashion, Coco Chanel, once said in her own defense: "How ridiculous wearing clothes by a man who doesn't know women, never had one, and dreams of being one!"

How were you to know your man was switch hitting? Besides, you met him at a vulnerable moment. There was this sister who had gone to school with a brother at Stowe Teachers College at St. Louis. She was popular among the heterosexual crowd and soon developed a relationship with a popular guy. The relationship was longlasting and presumed to end in marriage.

Then, after graduation she learned he'd fathered a child in his high school days and wasn't helping to support the child he'd kept a secret. Plus she didn't exactly want a ready-made family and didn't know whether she could trust this fellow after all or depend on him when and if the going got rough. She was afraid that what had happened to his high school flame might happen to her — and chances are she was right. Anyway, they went their separate ways, she taught in a small exurban town somewhere outside Kansas City.

Her first day at the school she ran into a male alumnus who'd already crossed her path quite a few times when he ran the student center during her first two years in college. He'd been so popular in his position at the place where all the students gather, she hadn't questioned his sexual orientation. The idea of homosexuality, let alone bisexuality, wasn't of much concern in that town in those days. As far as she knew, nobody else was suspicious of the fact he never had a steady girlfriend; and when he did date on major occasions such as Homecoming or the fraternity ball, his dates on reflection were merely ornamental, a member of the Homecoming Court, the Dean's daughter or something, not a lover, let alone a serious one.

Although she never thought it would mean anything to her and her own life, she knew in some vague way at least that in small-town communities in the Southern Farm Belt, young men weren't allowed to rise to the top among teachers or to pastor prestigious congregations or occupy "respectable" positions without taking somebody to the altar. After a while somebody would start to talk about them.

Nobody talked about "sexual orientations," but a lot of "bisexual" men (homosexual, if you ask me) resorted to marriage as a cover for a stable job. There weren't any men in earrings back then, no "eunuchs" as ideal social types. You were either masculine, unequivocally, or you were written off as a "sissy" and pushed to the side in everybody's romantic mind. So, though she never thought she'd marry the up-and-coming assistant principal from her campus, who'd been so popular in college, they were often brought together at school and community events, and he began to seem like a pretty good "catch." In those days people would start to call a woman an "old maid" if she wasn't married at 25.

She noticed when she announced her marriage some eyebrows went up. People who knew them both were subtle with their hints. Suddenly, they wondered aloud why they'd never seen this man with a woman before, couching it in backhanded compliments that she was his first love. They began to scrutinize his every mannerism for any feminine nuances. But she put it out of her mind and he passed the test and she married and had two children before she started to suspect that everything wasn't kosher in her household.

Before her depression and hospitalization materialized, her confusion led her one day to ask a doctor why she no longer appealed to her husband. She started to dress up and snuggle close to him in bed wearing voluptuous lingerie, but he kept turning his back on her. His road trips increased (for business purposes), unnecessary community meetings multiplied, along with a sudden variety of flimsy other reasons not to be left alone with her. She wondered sometimes, increasingly if he wanted to be with somebody else, but she never suspected it might be another man.

So, to sister friends who worry about the high rate of black males who are openly gay, believing they pose a sidewinding threat to the already dwindling male supply — to those who worry about the white woman — I'm here to tell you the person to watch out for is the bisexual brother, the one you think is heterosexual, the black Rock Hudson. Water eventually seeks its own level, and most people return to what they really are, what they believe will make them happy. So your competition is not only most likely to be within your race; he's within your handsome heartthrob's same gender. Your BMW's homosexual lover may very well know you, but you don't know him. You've heard a lot in recent years about the "Morehouse Man." Well, the other day, I was talking on the telephone to a Morehouse alumnus. Unsolicited by me, he started talking about the high rate of bisexuality in the world today. He revealed that the in-house word for Morehouse is "Whorehouse".

Let me give you some tips on how to know *him*. I'm not presenting them as any kind of infallible, foolproof formulas, nor as weapons to use to hit your past relations over the head. Nor are they invitations to enter the crippling shackles of a sexual paranoia or to be used as sinister searchlights in the service of meanspirited homophobia. Use them only for the high moral purposes of enlightened self defense. The life you save may be your own. However, if matters become too agonizing, it's a good idea to hurry over to a psychotherapist or marital counselor.

In the meanwhile, you can give him this casual litmus test:

1. You can sometimes judge a book by looking at the cover. Pay careful attention to the clothes the brother wears. I know this is the age of unisex fashions and men wear things they wouldn't have been caught in 15 years ago. In fact, you probably find it a wee bit odd that as soon as a little sun comes out, you arrive at the concert (or picnic or cookout or wherever you like to hang and chill where black people get together) to find more brothers in shorts than sisters.

2. This also isn't true of everybody, but (even though he's very

macho), after he starts to wear earrings and suddenly begins to buff his nails too. I recognize we're treading on somewhat complicated ground in our unisexual era, and a lot depends on the age of the brother. It's one thing when he's a young dude listening to gansta rap and into the adolescent peer group (he'll wear anything!), but it's another when he's 35 or 50.

3. He's into hairbraiding. Not that everybody into hairbraiding is bisexual. The last time I was in a beauty shop, an old fossil came in and revealed he'd just spent three hours getting his hair braided, that the cosmetologist was going to need another three hours to complete his colorful coiffure.

4. He's beginning to get more pedicures than you could imagine for yourself.

5. His eau de toilette suddenly starts to light up the room ahead of him.

6. He's past 39 but claims he hasn't been able to find a woman suitable for marriage. There may be a shortage of men but ain't no shortage of women. If he's got anything going for him, he'd have to be carrying a stick around to protect himself.

7. He's always talking about "this friend of mine" — but never allows you to meet him.

8. You've had six glorious months of dating and puppy love kissing, but he's never wanted to go to bed with you. Once when I was doing a seminar at a small midwestern college, a sister took the mike and preached on this for days. The sister broke it down to the practical guideline that, whether there's love in his heart or not, the average brother, no less than former

president Jimmy Carter, has lust in his heart or, at the very least, feels the need to say that he got over sexually. In most cases, all he wants is to score.

9. The company he keeps. Remember the saying, "Birds of a feather flock together." Most of his friends are fragile and generate questions about their orientation or lifestyle. (This is not to say that all effeminate men are gay or bisexual anymore than all football players and boxers are heterosexual). But we tend to select our friends and running buddies from among the persons we repeatedly bump into or share something in common with.

10. He's over 35 and still living at home with "mom", has never married. You mean this brother's a BMW, in the middle of the marriageable pool, eligible, and hasn't ever, one-little-second ever, been married? You better sniff around some more. Find out if, when, and who were the last girl friends he had. I mean this brother is pedigreed, has an M.D., or Ph.D., Ed.D., D.D., anything beside his BBD's and is never seen with a woman? If he says he can't find one, tell him to go next door and check out Tamika.

11. Let's face it, most single men want their own "pad", especially now that motels and hotels have become so expensive. Otherwise brothers want living quarters they can share with another brother who's also on the prowl, who's chasing after the same kind of prey. Their next inclination would be to "shack up" with *you*. This doesn't include everybody you know as these are hard economic times, and a large percentage of men — under 35, at least — have turned to living at home, if only because the break from the nest looks harder in the inner city maze these days.

Welfare sisters should be especially careful. Word is that you don't wish to risk losing your AFDC benefits and this could certainly happen if you marry. And, should you marry and say "to hell with the benefits, I have a BMW who loves me," there is always the nagging fear that the brother may soon take a powder — and you know how long it takes to start the benefits up again.

You'd be surprised by the number of black males who will play and prey upon your fears. One client came into the clinic, after having given up her food stamps for a BMW, bemoaning the fact that her man was using the social service policy as an excuse not to marry her. ("Baby, I would marry you tomorrow but you said you might lose your federal aid"). It used to be that you would have to hide your man to get your benefits. Now that social workers are afraid to go into the community, he can live in the house but can't be married to you. It could crop up in the social worker's computer files. However, if you live in a city such as San Francisco, you'd better ask around before you become involved with *any* brother).

12. He's never seen with a woman, let alone in a serious love or dating relationship.

13. One surefire test is this: If it acts like a duck, walks like a duck and quacks like a duck, it must be a bisexual duck.

Remember, when it comes to would-be BMWs, the brother may be black and beautiful and may well be working, but there may be some missing link, one that is easily overlooked, especially by a sister running up against her biological clock and fending off pressures from family, friend and foe who wonder aloud and signify as to when they'll be hearing "those wedding bells." So that, approaching the age of thirty — not to mention forty — some sisters panic and fall for anything wearing pants or holding down a job. They slip into gender denial, closing their eyes to their long-held standards of what is a man and what is a woman.

With desperation closing in, any avenue, any escape hatch, seems attractive. All the traits she once thought to be feminine in a man are now rationalized away as mere sophistication. To sisters who've been rocked to and fro and pummeled by crude mistreatment at the hands of a seemingly endless string of masculine cads, feminine qualities in a man may begin to seem "genteel." Which is where the bisexual brother comes in, slipping and sliding between the genders, operating from the vantage point of a two-pronged romantic repertoire, an intricate acquaintance with masculinity (his gender condition) and femininity (his practiced fantasy).

In a counseling seminar, a preacher friend who does pastoral counseling told of a woman in his congregation who was having second thoughts about continuing to date a bisexual brother. She was embarrassed by his switching, queenish public demeanor, and his late night creeping. The sister said that, nevertheless, she still had to be with this bisexual brother at least once a month, when she could always get some "sho nuff good lovin." "I guess because he's both man and woman," she explained.

So, if you don't want to get caught between a rock and a hard place, you've got to proceed with caution, which shouldn't be too troublesome if you'll subject your potential BMW ahead of time, from the get-go, to the thirteen warning signals of the Litmus Test. Then, if you even suspect something isn't altogether right with your BMW, you need to hurry to a counselor or do another Litmus Test screening to scrutinize your ambivalent impostor and remove his dainty cover.

Married Men

How often have you heard a sister say, she's dating a married man, because some other woman did it to her when she was married? "They didn't care how I felt. After all, *he's* the one that owes something to his wife — I don't".

She may also claim exoneration in the fact that she really doesn't call his house. "If I need to contact him, I know his number on the job. I have yet to become the kind of person who calls and hangs up in his wife's face."

Furthermore: "He's good to me. We take little trips on weekends. And he really goes all out for Christmas and birthdays. Besides, what she [his wife] doesn't know can't really hurt her."

Well expect what goes around to come around. If it becomes your good fortune to be the wife the next time around, instead of the other woman, don't be surprised when you get doubled-over by the same scenario. Men in marital therapy with wives who were once their girlfriends, complaining now about some other woman, sometimes tell such wives: "you knew I was doing that when I met you."

Even if you never wind up on the outside looking in, you may still be treading on hazardous turf. I remember a very prominent "bourgeois" lady in a midwestern town who was going with a married pillow of the community. They were and still are, last I heard, directors of Christian Education in their churches and attained head offices in district and statewide congresses requiring them to travel a lot together, attend the same functions, often out of town, almost always with lots of h'or douvres, food and refreshments. On top of that, they took up the practice of plotting secret getaways to rendezvous with champagne, for her, and brandy for him. Both fornicators were considerably overweight, especially the sister, and suffering from high blood pressure related to obesity and the stressful high lifestyle.

It came to pass that one amorous night in a hotel room, while the brother was on top of her doing his business, he suffered congestive heart failure and died on top of her, buck naked. The sister was petrified, momentarily frozen in fear, caught in a quandary of what to do, wondering what her family and church members would think, not to mention the pastor, as images of coroners and gossip columnists in black weekly newspapers floated across her mind. As rigamortis was creeping in, she was able to wiggle and wrestle herself out from under the brother and dial 911.

After calling close members of her family, she finally got her courage up to dial her lover's wife, with whom she was also personally well acquainted. The newspapers and rumor mills had a natural field day, as expected, and her children were shocked. Embarrassed and confused, they soon grew removed and distant, while she herself became more of a recluse than Greta Garbo.

Even if the brother hadn't died, the likelihood was that their relationship would have ended anyway. He would have left her sooner or later. When the married brother becomes divorced or widowed, he seldom marries the other woman, preferring to keep the situation as it is, to have his cake and eat it too, to continue to play around as he has done before.

At other times, once an affair with another woman is exposed, wifey turns on the heat, and he has to make a hurried choice. In most cases, your two-timer will disappear as fast as snowflakes in an electric chair.

This is why so many "other women" who are experienced in that role tend to avoid heavy pressure on their married lovers. Some even recommend throwing off suspicion by becoming friends with the brother's wife or at least friendly when and if you have to call. No time for getting an attitude or dropping catty hints or digs. In fact, calling the house or riling up the wife in anyway is a no-no of serious consequences. What makes the enterprise of loving a married man so perilous is, like crime or murder, it's high risk for a fatal slip-up.

Speaking of the church, a deacon I know in -- well, let's say the Seattle, Washington area — got into a thing with his church secretary. Mind you, this brother wasn't just any deacon, he was president of the deacons and one of the head honchos of the Board of Trustees. The pastor wouldn't think of making a move without consulting him. The young church secretary herself was moving on up, was already in charge of the missionary society, the pastor's guild, the outreach program, and seems she even had a couple of other coveted positions.

Turns out they both were sports addicts and followed the World Series among other things. His wife didn't like sports but had grown accustomed to this diversion on his part, so there was no problem explaining his absence on such occasions. The problem was his wife kept the budget and the receipts for the tax accountant, so was privy to any motels, fancy restaurant tipping, sneaking, creeping and anything else that didn't appear to be completely aboveboard, which made it strategic for the brother to use the other woman's credit cards and pay her the cash.

But one day on a cross-state sporting trip, the sister's cards were filled to the gills and the brother had to use his own. Meanwhile, the wife knew the motel he was going to use and told a couple of friends that she was going to surprise him and take some of his favorite foods to the motel.

Once there, she was informed by the registration clerk that the motel didn't give out room numbers of registered guests, so the wife presented her card to rent a room for herself, planning to call him from her room. When the card was placed in the machine, the computer showed the name and number to be correct. "Looks like you're already registered here, room 206." The motel clerk let her through and, luckily, the sister wasn't armed or violent, but there hasn't been that much lip around that motel in the current staff's memory.

The sister slung the soulfood she was carrying at both of them as they jumped up to run reaching for their clothes. She was able to stop the woman, one of her best friends, but her husband had run a little track in high school and got past her out the door, buck naked, leaving his wife (who wouldn't let the other woman have her clothes) fighting the other woman naked, in broad daylight. Meanwhile, he, the husband, was outside without a stitch of clothes on trying to flag a taxi cab. Another brother, driving a cab, passed by and threw him his coat, and yelled, "man put something over yourself."

The cops came along and picked up her husband and took him down to the General Hospital for observation and evaluation as to whether he was a danger to himself or others. The fight was stressful to this sister for two reasons: not only was it her husband, he was out with one of her best friends and one of her best friends was there with her man.

71

Quite often, you'll find when it's hard to keep your man at home, it's somebody you know that's making it hard. So watch your girlfriends. A lot of times the vibes are good between you and another lady precisely because of your commonality of tastes. The one who runs with you, knows you, likes the same things you like, lives the same lifestyle for the same reasons, talking it over with you all day long by phone and sometimes in the night, in an out of your house, is the one that's more like you.

Sometimes she's not your running buddy, only knows you casually. She may be the person who stands beside you in the choir. The one who works with you on the Usher Board. It could be your sorority sister, or some neighbor who knows your comings and goings and sometimes has the occasion to see and interact with you and the BMW you've got. They also hear you talking about your man, how good a man he is and all, and she wants the same thing.

All she needs is the gall to go with the wherewithal she has to take you out of the picture. She'll even tell you real quick, if you ever have the occasion to ask her, that she's "not that kind of woman." What she doesn't add is she's the kind that enjoys singing the song that says "he may be your man, but he wasn't your man last night."

If I Could Snap My Fingers

If I could snap
my fingers
and make everything
alright. . . .
 the show
 would have
 a new script
 you and I would be
 family everlasting
 no clock
 would be set
 for time departure
 and your walking
 out the door
 would bring no
 anguish to bear.
If I could snap
my fingers. . . .
 the one you're
 living with
 loving with
 building family with
 would be me.

© *Njeri H. Nuru*
Howard University

Brothers Who Play

A lot of brothers who aren't athletic will nevertheless want to play the "sporting life," to run around too late at night, propping themselves up as patrician sugar-daddies, pretending to be the last of the big spenders (sometimes with your money, or with some other woman's).

According to Dr. Jackie Jackson, a medical sociologist in Duke University's Department of Psychiatry, "black men who play [tend to be] those who are dysfunctional in their roles as husbands to black women or as fathers to their very own black children." Writing in a journal published by The Black Think Tank called *Black Male/Female Relationships,* Dr. Jackson went on to say that these brothers "include unwed, separated, and divorced fathers who could, but who do not 'pull their fair share' as economic providers for black mothers and children." But wait — there's more: "this operationalized definition," Dr. Jackson maintains, "could be extended to include politically influential black men who generally ignore the plight of black female-headed families residing in poverty, or who support federal policies and programs likely to keep such families in poverty through successive generations. Dr. Jackson suggests that "the consequences of men who play are far more detrimental on black families than are those which may be attributable to playing black women," but she admits that her assumption is open to "empirical testing."

Dr. Jackson sees storm clouds ahead for black people, in any case, and notes that black teenagers who used to refer to sexual intercourse as "making love" now prefer to speak of "making out." The sociologist bemoans particularly the "devil-may-care" attitude she sees among so many young black men today when it comes to women they get pregnant.

While admitting that she does not "have all the answers," Dr. Jackson says she knows enough to suggest that the need to "reduce the screwing of black families by black men who play" is an issue which should receive "high priority" in future discussions of black male/female relationships. She contends that it is a more "potent issue" than the issue of black males who desert black females for white women. Dr. Jackson's no-nonsense advice to the brothers: "stop the screwing." Sisters, help your brothers adhere to this simple sociological script, as it is sisters who at times contribute to the problem when they fall for brothers with enticing personalities and exciting characteristics who are smooth in the art of male/female interaction. Some may appear deceptively attractive because of the power and excitement suggested by their high social stature or lofty place in life.

I know that scientific research has demonstrated repeatedly that, throughout the animal kingdom, the female tends to imitate the choices of other females just as black men and people in general follow the fads or fashions of the peer group. But, Sister, you're going to have to begin to understand, that when these guys are playing around with a lot of women, they're not likely to stop their game with you. Well, maybe for a moment or two sometimes, but keep in mind that the brother who plays has picked up a whole lot of experience from a lot of different ladies, and he will probably keep on getting that experience for a long time to come. Some of it at your expense.

For example, from your first day on the job or wherever else you may concentrate your search for your BMW, avoid the brother who is always borrowing from his mother to take you out, let alone borrowing from you, borrowing some other brother's clothes, some other woman's car, or constantly crying to you about "running a little short." This brother is liable to be coming up short all his life.

Remember, the brother didn't become the MVP ("most valuable player") overnight. He who plays very well with you has probably played well with somebody else, or soon will, once he has conquered you. The brother who never keeps his commitments, is always running around with some other woman he tells you is his friend or something, is a brother you may need to tune out. Tune out the rap and take a good look at him, look beneath the surface of his skin, so to speak. Probe his cranium, his very lungs, his voice box, his gizzard. The brother's rap is his song. Try to imagine what will be left when the song is over. What will it be like when the music is no longer playing but you are left to linger with his rap and his jive.

Somebody should tell the potential BMW that if they "don't want to sleep in the harlot's bed, don't go near the harlot's door." Meanwhile, you can learn to know the difference immediately between a genuine BMW and another kind of brother, a black "main," as a lot of sisters call a man. Unlike the BMW, this brother will often mean you no earthly good and will want to use you in a lot of different ways to try to prove his mythical so-called sexual superiority.

The search for manhood or compensatory masculinity is also something that feeds the myth or the stereotype of black male sexual superiority. I'm not saying the black man isn't sexually superior, and I'm not saying that he is. I can't say I rightly know. But I do know that the black male excels in athletics and the black male excels in dancing, and sex is a form of both athletics and dancing. You can draw your own conclusion, but let Anne do her own research.

When I was a radio announcer for a San Francisco station that was carrying the games of two professional teams, the Giants and the 49ers (in fact, O.J. was then on the 49ers team and baseball hall-of-Famer Willie McCovey was with the Giants), I frequently overheard white female employees whispering about the "beautiful, narrow, tight butts" of the black ballplayers.

These race-conscious lady belles, some of Southern origin and some married with fullgrown children, could hardly ever contain themselves whenever they could watch ballplaying brothers walking up and down the station corridors. One day, in fact, O.J. brought Nicole with him to a business meeting. We all sat there open-mouthed as department heads in our workaday business suits, getting ready to receive one of our most famous ballplayers in the world.

Finally, in strolls Nicole wearing skinnylegged jeans. As soon as the meeting started, she kicked off her shoes (she wore no stockings) and propped her feet up in O.J.'s lap. O.J. sat stroking Nicole's bare feet throughout the meeting, impervious to the sumptuous, bounteous catered spread of Danish rolls, bagels, lox, and Philadelphia cream cheese with Nicole grinning, squirming, purring, and slinging her hair.

Even now, this very moment, as I write, word just came in to me that a certain darkskinned baseball hall-of-famer who also used to parade through the radio station as a member of the San Francisco Giants is now shacking up with a blondish peroxide (of course) television reporter on a local San Francisco Bay Area television station.

The stereotypes of black male sexuality have clearly whetted the white woman's curiosity quite a bit (at the same time as they have combined with the new sexual demands the white woman has

77

made on the white man, driving up his impotency rate). Brothers meanwhile have appeared to internalize these stereotypes themselves and, much too frequently, will manifest them shamelessly in openly flirtatious pursuits of the white woman in public places in broad daylight and in superstud games with white *and* black women both. This is why you have to try to help your BMW understand the difference between sexual manhood and true social manhood, or tell him to get to stepping.

Proving his manhood. It goes without saying, as you may already know, that the challenge of the male (and the source of his anxiety in the sexual encounter) arises in the need to gain and hold an erection. As blues singer Big Joe Turner used to say, "don't get me nervous, woman, I'm holding a baseball bat in my hand."

The ability of a man to attract a woman may pivot more on his social potency (his wealth, prestige, eminence or power) than on his physical and personal charms — for instance, Spike Lee, Snoop Doggy Dog and Whitney Houston's Bobby Brown can be sex objects, but not Oprah Winfrey or Gladys Knight. The black male suffers an ambiguity, a double whammy. Blocked from the avenue to social potency (social power or position), he is frequently impelled to overcompensate in the sexual.

This is the reason so many brothers in a hope-to-die romantic struggle with their woman, may be inclined to seek refuge in the waiting arms of a multiplicity of other women. But this only hampers the brother's ability to make the struggle with any one woman. By contrast, many sisters moving on up the social ladder, will find themselves affluent without a man while brothers will be broke with too many women. It used to be that you could walk through the black community and see a lot of working men and a lot of pretty women. Now you see a lot of working women and a lot of pretty men at home.

Many black men will cultivate a conspicuous masculinity in their physical bearing, making their very walk a bouncing jive cat jitterbug kind of strut or shuffle. While the white man is inclined to sit in somewhat of an effeminate posture — legs crossed, arms folded, or with hands clasped over the knee, the black man prefers a posture with legs ajar, reminiscent of a bullfrog ready to leap, opened decidedly wider than would be expected of a woman, leaning forward in a way to look as menacing as he can.

This means that you will have to be on guard against your man's masculinity needs, his "manhood." I'm not just talking about things like Johnny Taylor's "take care of your home work, girl, because if you don't somebody will." I mean you can't take it too personal or get your dandruff up when your man gets to complaining about somebody stepping on his "manhood." You may have to "massage his ego" a tiny little bit before you drag him off to the dishpan or the mop bucket. Don't be too quick to think he's just a whining weakling when he wails about "the man," or too quick to take the other side when he rants against "the system." Don't inadvertently become his psychological enemy when you could be a steady leaning post. On the other hand, you've got to learn how to differentiate between your role as confidant or listener, and the need to set some kind of limits to his crying on your shoulder.

Massaging the masculine ego can be a touchy matter, often perilous, because experience has taught too many black men to feel their manhood compromised at almost every turn, in virtually everything they do or try to do and everywhere they go. Remember, in a white-dominated society, it is the oppressed male, not the female, who poses the primary threat to the ruling male. It is the black male who in the white male's mind can take his place in the bedroom as well as the boardroom. It is this quality of hurt that too often seduces a black male to try to prove his manhood through his penis or use his penis as a weapon of intersexual warfare standing idling his youth away, hanging on the corner with one hand cupping his sexual region as if checking to see if it's still there.

Sleep-In Lovers And The Man Over Your Children

You've heard of monogamy (married to one person) and polygamy (married to one person too many). Well, it seems we're living now in a time when many are moving into "omnigamy" (where everybody is just about married, has been, or soon will be marrried to just about everybody else). But leaving all jokes aside, when you consider that 67 per cent of children born to black women 18 to 44 years old are born to single women, not to mention children already born to previous mates or husbands, an awful lot of sisters are going to have to learn how to deal with a situation where the man over her children isn't their natural father.

When you were a child, you probably sometimes overheard your mother and other elderly women talking, especially when they didn't know you were around or exactly listening to what they were saying. "If something ever happens to LeRoy, I ain't never go'n bring no man in here over my kids." Or: "I ain't go'n get married again til these kids get grown." This attitude, these apprehensions, were especially acute where daughters were concerned, for fear of sexual molestation or related hanky panky. (It's now to the point, in places such as San Francisco, L.A. and New York City, where many anxious sisters are getting afraid of the sexual molestation of their *sons* by their stepfathers.)

However, in cases where the natural father is deceased, quite a few of the women who vow never to marry again or even take on a serious relationship over their children out of a wish to shield them from potential abuse by a man who is not their father, are motivated mainly by the feeling that neighbors and church friends expect them to remain true to the memories of their husbands. But many also fear their daughters may be in sexual peril from the men

81

in their lives. And it is true that, for men who haven't quite matured, despite advancing age — who are caught up in a perennial pursuit of younger women — your daughter may represent a "youthful you." She may embody, in a most enticing way, a provocation of fantasies of what your figure and energy level used to be to your man. In his often unconscious endeavor to cling to his eroding youth, he may grow attracted to your daughter.

These days especially, a growing girl may flit and flounce about the house half-naked. On your man's way to the bathroom, for instance late in the night, he may notice her careless hips sleeping in teddies or an over-sized shirt with nothing under them, not covering her bare legs and breasts.

A sister I know on the other side of town once married a man a few years younger than herself. Wrinkles already were creeping into her face and people were beginning to notice her plump and sagging jowls. It was in this context that her husband would switch and sway to her daughter's rap music but turn around and swear he never heard of any of the dances he used to do with her mother or "oldies but goodies" they used to sing. The more sister-friend had to soak her feet from a hard day's work (and a little age), the more he tapped his feet to her daughter's music.

One night she came home from work to find that her man was having an affair with her seventeen-year-old daughter. What's more the daughter, two months short of eighteen, openly swore her love for the man and, when the mother put the Negro out, in two weeks her daughter followed him.

You've got to keep in mind that, far more than a biological father, a stepfather is subject to drop his guard against the idea of sexual transgression, and this impulse may slip up on him in a gradual way. Remember, this man watching your daughter develop as a woman has no blood relationship to her and, in most cases never knew or lived with her before her sexuality began to bloom.

On the other hand, some women, losing their figure and their youthful features as father time draws near, may also think of their daughter on some level as a representative of themselves at an earlier age. This may even generate a sense of competition and resentment vis-a-vis their daughter, who certainly will become the "other woman" in a most horrific way if she should happen to fall victim to your lover man's sexual curiosity.

This may be one of the reasons mothers are so frequently given to denial in these situations. They're reluctant to confront the feelings of rejection and hurt, the thought that her man sought somebody else, above all her daughter. Not to mention the embarrassment when it comes to the open attention of family, friends and neighbors. Then, there's also the frequent feeling of obligation to break up the marriage and leave the man you may truly love. In this era of the black male shortage, many women understandably would rather pretend it isn't so. You've seen these stories and testaments on the daytime "talkies" where sometimes it's brought to light, on the other hand, that daughters cry foul for their own reasons.

But often when a daughter is raped or molested by a stepfather, her mother may actually realize it's true but choose to turn a deaf ear and look away and otherwise pretend not to believe their child. In cases where the child is telling the truth, this causes the girl not to get the counseling she may need and, frequently, to arrive at the door of adulthood with a lifetime of resentment and ambivalence toward her mother as well as her stepfather or molester.

So, an ounce of prevention is generally better than a pound of cure. When I was growing up in Tulsa, Oaklahoma, I used to hear old women warning one another, "don't leave your daughter with your husband while you're gone to Texas to visit your momma. People will talk about her."

I used to wonder "why would they talk about *her?*" I now realize that the custom was an unconscious means of prevention, that it circumvented any necessity to condemn any individual man in advance or even to cast unwarranted suspicion on his character. The possibiltiy for onus is placed on public perception of the girl, who is the one in need of protection — in advance, not restitution after victimization, to punish a deed when it's done, which still wouldn't undo the fact that a girl has been molested.

While we're at it, sisters, make your daughter put something on when she's flouncing around the house. This will present to her a simultaneous opportunity to learn the fundamental canons of modesty and feminine deportment. Now is the time for her to begin to realize that she can't sit on daddy's knee as recklessly or as wantonly as she did before. Now is the time to develop a certain amount of separation or individuation from the father, the opposite-sexed parent. Just as an adolescent boy cannot massage his mother's breasts the way he did when nursing as an infant or tot, or put his hands on her hips at will, neither can a daughter straddle her father's lap and wiggle around as she did when she was a toddler. Welcome to the laws and inner workings of human sexuality.

Many mothers caught in the middle of a molestation of their daughers by their husbands are blinded by the psychological mechanisms of denial, as I said earlier. I have a friend who is a retired social worker who operates a couple of group homes for foster children. She often tells me of kids their mothers "put out" in preference for the man.

One little girl, a five year old, had been raped by her step-father who was babysitting her in the summer while her mother worked. After the authorities had seized the child, the mother continued to live with the stepfather. Some years later they divorced and she married somebody else. However, after years of psychotherapy and court deliberations, the girl eventually was returned to her mother but, at thirteen, was raped by her new stepfather. The girl's mother was furious. She angrily scolded and chastised the girl, telling her it wasn't enough that she had flirted with her first stepfather when she was five years old; now she had tempted this stepfather too.

On the other side of the coin, I understand from a forensic psychologist I know, who sometimes treats parents accused of child abuse by social workers, that it is not unusal for a social worker to tell a mother: "you can get the kids back right now if you would get rid of your husband."

So, listen to this: don't leave your daughter alone with your man and unprotected for long periods of time, and you will never have to worry. Misunderstanding this these days, we've gone into an attitude of "do-your-own-thing," "let-it-all-hang-out," when feminists get on television in mini-skirts drawn almost to their hips, complaining of "sexual harassment" and mouthing self-righteous but naive preachments of "male responsibility." In reality, it is society that has the responsiblity, to male and female alike. But if a people that refuses to learn from its history is doomed to repeat it, a people that refuses to learn from its elders may soon have no history to repeat.

Take the matter of spanking, of discipline, something that served us well for thousands of years but now has been demeaned, diminished and all but discarded as "corporal punishment." Remember the peach tree that used to be in the backyard when you were growing up? It was out there, as you seemed to know instinctively, from the time you were a toddler, it was out there to do more than bear fruit. On Sunday, remember how you'd be sitting in the church acting up, but all your mother had to do was glance in your direction. It was a glance that said "don't let me have to come over there."

Every once in a while you had a fool, even in the black family, who would challenge their mother's glance. As soon as you got home from church, you were sent straight to the back yard to get a switch. And if you brought in something that was too short you were considered in open defiance. If you could get back out there, past the belt or ironing cord or whatever correctional paraphernalia was available to straighten you out, it would be explained to you later that, one day in life "you'll learn to always remember the bridge that brought you safely across."

This was before integration brought disintegration to the black family and institutional life, before white social workers and civil libertarians came to tell us we were "beating" our children. Parents would say, "if I don't straighten you out now, the cops will when you're sixteen.

When we look at what we have now, our parents were prophetic. I'm not advocating that you actually beat your children, but wouldn't it be wonderful if the people that we don't tell how to raise their children, the people who raised Boy George, wouldn't tell us how to raise ours? As things now stand, discipline may be the touchiest issue of all that will come into the relationship between a man and his stepdaughter. Here again, the old tradition of the father not hitting or disciplining the daughter, as well as the sexual division of labor in parenting, may apply and may be why it's sometimes said that "it takes a woman to raise a daughter and man to raise a son."

In some tribes on the continent of Africa (and even in black rural Southern communities before we got "integrated" and sometimes disintegrated), the custom prevailed of leaving the discipline of the girls to the mother and the boys to the father. This allows a parent automatically to teach by example, in fact to become a built-in role model for the child that he or she seeks to discipline. Also and equally, it sidesteps a certan amount of induced hostility and animosity between a child and the opposite-sexed parent.

One thing that plagues male/female relationships among a people where so many fathers are gone from the home or remain largely unavailable psychologically to the children, even when in the home, is what pschoanalysts call the "cupboard syndrome."

Boys in such a circumstance are more likely to grow up seeing the mother as a cupboard, a repository of food, nurturance, goodies and gratification, but also a bit excessive in her role as single parent, the person who has to whack the boy's hand out of the cookie jar and otherwise curb his hand. Many such boys grow up to regard their mates as extensions of their mother and to fight out with their mates the unresolved hostilities and conflict left over from their childhood struggles with their mother.

This raises a certain contradiction, a complication of the early need to reinforce the stepfather's validity as a full and functional parent in the lives of your childen, the need to allow the stepfather to be as authoritative as they are caring of your children. However, once a girl begins to come of age, the stepfather (indeed the father) is no longer to whip her, let alone to spank her on the buttocks, for fear he may confuse himself on some dark rainy night when the six-pack of malt liquor has loosened his impulse-control — especially while you're out with the girls or serving the community more than you serve your man's sexual needs There may already be an element of hostility between you and your daughter, while she's close and cuddly with her father figure.

I know a woman now in her mid-forties who still cries about the times she was slapped by her stepfather. One day, her mother told her stepfather, "if you ever put your slimy hands on her again, I'll kill your narrow ass."

Not that the stepfather isn't entitled to full parental rights. In fact, this situation should have been anticipated and talked about in private long before it even had a chance to happen. Because of the psychological stages in the making of a woman (or a man for that matter), something appropriate, if not essential, in an early stage may no longer be appropriate and may even be dysfunctional.

I don't want to give stepfathers a bad name. As a matter of fact, your casual boyfriend may be more likely than a stepfather to commit transgressions or sexual misconduct. For one thing, you've usually had a chance to know a man you married longer and you're more likely to have worked out rules and regulations in relation to the children. Many women, in fact, may unwisely follow a policy of never bringing a man home. She thereby robs her children of a natural emotional experience and the opportunity to learn the ways of man and woman by example. She distorts their image of her relationships and ultimately their own.

It's at this point that we have succeeded in mounting the tightrope of ambivalence in the interaction of your man and your children. On the one hand, we have the stepfather who is truly treacherous or at least unaccepting and evil to a woman's children that are not his own. But you and I know that there are many black men who make wonderful stepfathers, manytimes better in fact than their natural fathers, who may not only be gone and gone for good but no-good and better gone. He's the kind of brother about which no news is good news.

Let's give the good guys a round of applause. Give it up for the good guys. Give all the good guys a standing ovation. In any case, let me remind you how important it is to validate over and over again, the parental authority and authenticity of the good stepfather, or the new stepfather you expect to be good in the minds of your children. Then, try to keep up a united front with him, because children already may be poised to view the stepfather as some kind of intruder, if not a homebreaker, the obstacle to their fantasies and secret dreams of the return of their father. They naturally wish to exploit the opportunity to drive a wedge into any disciplinary crack. "You ain't my father" is an almost inevitable response of such children to any unwanted stance on the part of a stepfather. Many women may have to fight their own ambivalence toward the stepfather's endeavor to assume the father's role.

Many men in clinical treatment complain that women want them to love their children like a father but not to enjoy the rights and privileges of the father, especially when it comes to setting rules, boundaries and discipline. This weakens the child's respect for the man of the house as well as the role of a man in the family, and it is something that may follow the child in their own adulthood love lives.

That's why I believe it's often a good strategy, as early as possible in the relationship, to encourage the stepfather to adopt the children, especially if there's no child support from your ex and many of the children grow up to regard their stepfathers as their psychological fathers — especially those whose natural fathers were never known or seldom if ever came around.

Hopefully you are one of those who luckily or wisely will choose such a jewel of a man. In the meantime, it may be advisable for you to recall and remember some of the old "over-the-clothes-line-wisdom," and begin to watch what you bring in over your children.

The Violent Man

There will come a time in most relationships when a man will want to jump violent, or at least will threaten to teach you a lesson, saying he'll "do a Mike Tyson on your so-and-so," if you keep fooling with him.

Many young brothers come of age in mean inner city streets, seeing men fighting women, manytimes their mothers, behind closed doors and sometimes up and down the street. Though it's no excuse for violence, the fact remains that sisters also come through these circumstances and situations and learn on the deepest level just what buttons to push to "tick a man off." Many believe, as they will tell you, that "true love never runs smooth," that good, good loving can only go with storming and raining and a whole lot of trouble, often played out to a background of gut-bucket blues "busting loose" over boisterous boom boxes and get-down ghetto blasters, punctuated by occasional pistol bullets, if you don't watch out.

Psychoanalysts are sometimes moved by this predicament to assert the existence of a kind of "feminine masochism" in the personality structure of certain poor women, and many brothers who claim to know the streets will propose to hide behind the notion that "a bitch ain't happy if she ain't getting her ass kicked sometimes."

Honey, let me tell you, you ain't in the streets, and you know how to come in out the rain. And those of you in the streets, come on out right now, because you won't find a BMW (Black Man Working) anywhere in the streets. You might find one working on the streets, i.e. construction, taxi, bus, subway, 'cause if they're in the streets they're playing, pimping, hustling and getting ovah. Just as luxury cars called BMWs are more likely to be parked in some garage than in the streets. Even before they had cars, let alone luxury cars of a modern vintage, the old black sages of the South who sat around quilting and gossiping or holding up the whittler's bench were quick to warn you: "If you don't call a halt to this the first time, child, you're in for a hard life." They'd say, "what you begin with, is what you'll end with."

An improbable figure to do so in the minds of many, Minister Louis Farrakhan recently told an all-black-female audience in Atlanta about his own short experience with the strategy of wifebeating when he was a young calypso singer living in New York. At one point in his lecture, the Minister confessed to his momentarily stunned listeners that he once hit his wife, Khadisha, who also was in the audience. "Then she hit me back and that was the end of that."

Whereas black women aren't inclined to do what Rita Bobbitt did, with or without a black male shortage, we're not into castrating, cutting off penises. But I can tell you one thing, if a sister ever did, they'd never be able to find it and sew it back on like they did with John Bobbitt.

I sat on a jury a few years ago where the white jurors and court officers, who didn't know anything about the black experience, were trying a sister for pouring a hot skillet of grease on her old man. The only other black person in the room beside me was the defense attorney. During the course of the deliberations, it was revealed that the black woman, the defendant, had been married to her man for more than a quarter of a century and had been in and out of the relationship. Through a special program, she had managed to get to Vassar but, still trying to stick by her man, was currently residing in the projects with the brother she had scalded after he jumped on her and slapped her around and pushed her down the steps. At the time of the trial, she had already spent about six months in jail awaiting trial, and by then the brother's scars had healed and were no longer visible, but he was pressing charges anyway.

A week or two after the verdict of "not guilty" had been rendered (because I hung the jury), I happened to run into the prosecuting attorney, who turned out to be a neighbor living down the street. One day when I was passing by, he told me "the judge said sometimes one or two vocal persons will lay back to hang the jury." I don't know who told him it was me. Maybe the defense lawyer or one of the jurors.

The prosecutor was very perturbed and demanded to know "how could you let somebody off who'd heated grease and poured it on her husband?" He seemed shocked when I said jokingly she'd "been heating that grease for twenty-five years." "How can you heat grease for twenty-five years?" He was puzzled. I told him "that's what happens when white folk try black people without knowing the black experience" and kept on going.

I've been interested in this issue since my husband and I were running Kupenda (Swahili for "to love") groups in the late 1970s and, hearing the commentaries and confessionals of wifebeaters and battered women discussing what had come to be called "battered woman's syndrome." In fact, we included an article, "How to Deal with a Violent Male," in the first issue of the journal we began publishing in 1979, *Black Male/Female Relationships.*

I remember that a sister wrote in and said: "My husband of five years of happy — blissful — marriage recently slapped me. I was horrified, for I grew up watching my mother beaten by my stepfather and swore I'd never stand for it myself. But I love my husband, and we have two wonderful, joyful children who love my husband, too. What makes a man fight a weak, defenseless woman?"

The answer was published as part of the article in *Black Male/Female Relationships*, explaining that "violence against a woman by a man has long been tabooed but too often tolerated in fact. In some social circles men even can be heard to claim openly that a woman isn't really happy unless she is 'chastised' now and again.

"Men (and women) who grew up watching their mothers fought by their fathers or other lovers may have come to feel, on some deep level in spite of themselves, that violence is the natural course of love and lovemaking. Fortunately, this idea is no longer socially acceptable, or at least has changed for the better, but psychological needs and habits die slowly. Politics is one thing, and the psychology of the individual can in one sense be another, lagging far behind his consciousness.

"Violence, when not sanctioned by subtle canons of women's subordination or macho posturing, is often a last-ditch defense on the part of a man who is experiencing a crisis in his masculine self-esteem.

"According to psychiatrist Sherwyn Woods, writing in a recent issue of the *Archives of General Psychiatry,* violence is an attempt to restore the lost esteem or loss of face through an aggressive act or demonstration of power and strength. At the same time, the violent man denies his infantile feelings of dependency and the passivity usually linked in his mind and in our society to the idea of the feminine. You don't say so," the letter continued, "but your husband could be currently undergoing some period of stress in life — loss of employment, approaching middle age, and doubts about waning masculine vigor, severe weight gain and midriff spread, a plummeting career, financial worries — which threaten his capacity to uphold his picture of himself as a person — in this case, as

94

a man.

"You must be on guard to avoid falling into his fears or aggravating them. At the same time, you must make it as clear as you can that violence is intolerable and that it adds nothing to your overall admiration and respect for him and his abilities.

"In the power struggle between man and woman, impulses to violence may be expected, and it is okay to have the urge to violence so long as it is not acted upon. Violence, in fact, is sometimes a feature of poor ability to control impulses and can be mixed with a pathological rage in explosive individuals who are quick to resort to violence with men and women. Sometimes it is aggravated by rigid masculine codes of how a woman should "behave," where losing an argument or conflict with the woman he loves is thought by a man to be "unmanly." Some men find relief from a heated argument by taking a long, slow walk, reflecting and cooling off. Others begin to realize that it is not necessary to win every battle to win the war or keep their pride, let alone to maintain their masculinity. In fact, a truly strong man is strong enough to be "weak" sometimes, to drop or discard the iron armor of feigned superiority.

"Violence against a woman, in any case, is an admission of defeat, an admission by the man that he is not holding his own, or able to hold his own by other means; as violence, except for the sadist or the psychopath, is a means of last resort.

"However, in the love-hate passion of romantic entanglements, the fact remains that one of the persons most likely to kill you is your mate. This arises from the old law of social conflict. Whenever hostility breaks out between persons, the more intimate the relationship (other things being equal), the more intense the hostility. Add to that the fact, when we choose a lover or a mate, we tend to choose someone to complement our ego ideal; in a round-about way, Freud says, we are choosing ourselves. When your 'better half' has done you wrong, deceived or hurt you, it is on some level a part of your 'self' that has injured the other (lesser?) half.''

I concluded that ''violence is virtually never a lasting solution to anything, particularly in a marriage; it usually reflects a failing relationship (though it need not fail) and a man's broken or fragile ego. I maintain that individual or couples therapy may be indicated and can help.''

As heinous and humiliating as it must be to have a husband slap your face, let alone do permanent damage to your features, domestic violence is a complicated matter, involving at least two individuals, and it is important that we do not let white feminists use us to take their agenda forward, as the National Organization for Women is doing in the O.J. Simpson case. We must be careful that our solutions must grow out of our own problems and our own circumstances. White people in general and white women in particular are using us these days for their own agendas. I believe I mentioned that blacks are usually named as the perpetrators of all the social ills going down now — from Clarence Thomas (sexual harassment), Mike Tyson (date rape), Marion Barry (corruption in politics), Michael Jackson (pedaphilia), to O.J. Simpson (domestic violence).

Sisters, when white men are guilty of similar mischief, we hardly hear a peep from them, let alone us. We didn't comment on Ted Kennedy at Chappaquiddick, who remains in the U.S. Senate, though Adam Clayton Powell was drummed out of Congress; William Kennedy Smith (date rape), who's now practicing medicine while Mike Tyson practices pushups. Senator Packwood is still in

96

the Senate, and Bill Clinton won't have to face Mrs. Jones until he's out of office. Marion Barry is back in office only because black working people outnumbered and outvoted whites and black bourgies in the District of Columbia.

It's not that I condone drug addiction, but I also know there are two kinds of politicians, those who're caught and those who're not caught. If the problems of black women are different, our solutions will be different and will have to be worked out by ourselves and in our own way.

Confessions Of An Ex-wife Beater

I beat her
because she loved me
I beat her
gouged my fingers
in her eye
stomped her
on the floor
because she loved me
because she loved my dirty drawers
I beat her
put my hands on her throat
squeezed until her eyes
looked like marbles
I beat her
because she loved me
because she gave me a child
that looked like me
because I held her hand
as our seed came forth
I beat her
because she wouldn't give me
some pussy
I beat her
tore her panties off
and took the pussy
then beat her
then said to her,
'I love you, baby, I love you
I love you so much
you're so precious to me
Let me kiss you.'
And she let me, then I beat her
for letting me
because I was drunk
too much rum
I beat her
too much weed
I beat her
too much coke
I beat her
My 'your're so precious to me'
I beat her

My, 'I love you so much baby'
I beat her
Because she was faithful
because she was patient
because she was
I beat her
while my child stood terrified
I beat her
kicked her
sat on her
punched her in the mouth
In my madness
because she said the wrong word
because she said nothing
because she said the right word
because she had a thought
independent of mine
I beat her
knocked her to the floor
because she called the police
I beat her
how could she
call the white man on me
as black as I was
because she called her mama
I beat her
because she called the operator
I beat her
because she picked up the telephone
I beat her
because she left me
and I found her
hiding in the closet
I beat her
because I took her to New York
and she didn't smile
I beat her
and when I got well
When I stopped beating her
she packed her bags, packed her baby
and left forever.

© By Marvin X

98

The Blue Collar Lover

My husband and I were asked by *Ebony* some years ago to offer suggestions for an article they were doing on "How Black Women Can Deal with The Black Male Shortage." Unlike some of the panel of experts, I suggested that — despite the black man shortage — giving men a license to have harems is not the solution to the problem.

I advocated that black women should take the same approach to finding a man as they take when looking for a job, a house or a car. Number one, establish your goals. Two, set a time frame, a deadline. Three, scout the market. And, four, make your selection.

And don't be afraid to let people know you're looking for a man, just like you would if you're looking for a house. Funny how we tell them when we're looking for a condo, you'd say, "Girl, I'm looking for a condo — and don't put me in the wrong part of town. "I want a good zip code." Or: "I'm looking for a job, one where I can move up, with all the perks, and a company car. Let me send you my resume."

I once met a college instructor, a black woman in her thirties on the faculty of a small college in a small Texas town where most of the men were married and dating students wasn't socially acceptable or personally desirable to her, especially since they were generally so much younger. She was in the San Francisco Bay Area visiting an old college chum from her undergraduate days, but it was clear also that she had come looking for fun and, possibly, the beginning of something exciting.

At the end of her vacation, I saw her one day looking down

and disappointed. None of her romantic expectations had materialized. She complained that the few black men her hostess knew were either married, gay, or not overly interested in black women. I told her to go back home to Texas and "drop her bucket" right there in the Texas wells. After explaining that many sisters (influenced by media hype and encouraged by too many selfserving brothers) tend to exaggerate the black male shortage in their own minds and the minds of the brothers, I suggested that, shortage or not, all she needs is *one* marriageable black male.

I told her to go home and take her address book and write down the names of all of her single girl friends, which she did. Since I'd advised her not to tell them of her hidden agenda, because many women, while thinking nothing of asking one another to help them to find a job or a condo or a special pair of shoes, feel somehow deeply embarassed to say, "hey, somebody help me; I'm looking for a man."

Anyway, ten of her girlfriends showed up. After they were settled comfortably into their screwdrivers and bloody marys, she handed out a pen and a pad to each of them and asked them to list every single black male that they knew anywhere around there. There was only one requirement: they had to be men in which they personally had no romantic interest. Of course, they were instructed to omit any known rapists, alcoholics, sociopaths, drug addicts, derelicts and social dysfunctionals.

The list grew longer and longer with the laughter. She collected all the pads and drew lines through any duplications. She was able to cull twenty eligible brothers. The next step was to have a gathering of the men and the women, which she did, and I was told that a lot of good things came out of the party, the details of which we'll leave to your imagination. But I'm happy to say that,

100

in addition to her own marriage, three of the other women were engaged in a couple of years, and I heard later that three of the others had met eligible men when they went out on dates with the guys garnered from the list in one way or another. In all cases where this idea has been tried, the news of showers, engagements, weddings and christenings have flooded my mailbox.

The need to update our manhunting strategy first occurred to me around 1980 when the issue was being debated whether black women set their standards too high. Although I didn't think they did (certainly black women deserve the best and should also demand that black men do their best by them), it's easy in a broken patriarchy to make the mistake of losing sight of certain realities, including the persistent shortage of black men at the top of the totem pole. You can't set your standards too high, but they can certainly be unrealistic. There's nothing wrong with wanting kings and the titled gentry, but where is *your* crown? Where is *your* dowry, Where is *your* lineage?

We can also make the mistake elaborated upon by Professor William Burgest of Governor State University in a book we edited, *The Crisis in Black Sexual Politics*. Black women *and* black men tend to seek out and choose one another on the basis of white standards. For his part, the black male too often puts black women at a handicap by choosing a woman according to how closely she approximates European physical features — clearly something black women will generally not possess in particular abundance. But black women also put black men at a handicap in choosing a man according to how closely he approximates social characteristics of the white male.

We may have to begin to change our values without lowering our standards. There're other qualities in a man besides his bank balance. There's such a thing as personality — and don't mention character. And I know you're saying "that doesn't pay the rent." "It doesn't pay the car note, and it doesn't keep the heat in the furnace in the wintertime, nor the air flowing in summer."

Just as we want the males to change their values, we may have to modify our own cash register mentality. If money is all you want, the dope dealers and number runners are out there waiting, along with the pimps and the shakedown artists. Too often we go looking for dollar signs but ignore many things that may prove to be of greater value to a lasting and satisfying relationship.

I won't bore you with all the lofty qualities you can get from self-esteem workshops, motivational speakers, self-help manuals, spiritualists and tea leaf gurus. I'll just get right down to basics. Take the matter of sex. When they speak of the sexual superiority of the black male, they're not talking about the middle class professional. They're not talking about your average college professor, your case worker, your school teacher, your elected/appointed officials. Not even the preacher. They're talking about the underclass male, the brothers in the hood, the dropout, the disenchanted, the gangbanger, the breakdancer, the gambler, the hustler and the ex-felon.

Incidentally, I have often heard both underlcass brothers and sisters in the clinic equate black professional men generally with "faggots." They don't mean that they're homosexual, just effeminate by the standards and codes of the streets.

Quiet as it's kept, the biggest pool of untapped black males can be found in the blue collar occupations. Yet a lot of sisters who don't mind having these brothers as secret, discreet lovers or sexual companions on the side, slipping in and out of their living quarters, unbeknownst to their bourgeois professional friends (who themselves may be doing the very same thing), many fail to see the full potential of this copious pool of marriageable black males.

Blue collar brothers include policemen, firemen, construction workers, bus drivers, cab drivers, postal workers (not just mail carriers, but mail clerks, UPS, Fed Ex, Airborne Express, whatever flies out there). We realize that not all of them have college degrees, but they have stable, well-paying salaries, good benefits if not the corporate perks, good hospitalization and dental plans, retirement plans (and they may be more likely to stay at the job long enough to actually get retirement someday). They're not easily fired, at least in the case of those in the civil service system, where it takes almost an act of Congress to remove them.

Unfortunately, a lot of bourgeois sisters have shied away from these brothers for the simple reason that they are afraid their friends will talk about them behind their backs. I once knew a young physician who lived in a sizable city in the Southwest. She was an aide to the state's director of public health. Her marriage to another physician was on the rocks when she met a hairstylist. She wanted to accept his proposal of marriage after her own divorce was final, but declined when friends told her, "how could you? This man won't fit into your circles. You're a doctor; he's a hairdresser. You can't be introducing your husband as a hairdresser!!" They began to whisper behind her back: "How can she stand that blue collar niggah? I couldn't be married to no blue collar niggah," the gossip went. And the band played on. When her mother, who was also an M.D. (her father was a lawyer), joined the chorus of disapproval, she bowed to the pressure and moved away from the city.

By the time she recovered — bless Pat — she ran into a young minister of the gospel, who was the assistant pastor of a modest church (which some might call a storefront) in the city in which she was living. She got flack from people about the minister too, but he did have a college degree, though no pedigree, and that too was whipped to her again by her Greek-lettered friends. But having given up the hairdresser already, she resolved to marry the preacher, living on a level of unhappiness over regrets that she hadn't thrown caution (and the advice of her girlfriends) to the wind and married the hairdresser in the first place, who, she was now hearing, had married one of her passing acquaintances who had cranked up the rumor mill that destroyed her chances with the hairdresser.

So don't you overlook the possibilities of a blue collar lover. Be on the lookout the next time you come across a postal employee, or some other government worker who's proud of his achievements, even if he doesn't have a high school diploma. He can learn. Your prospective BMW may be found in the church, right under your nose.

He's doing alright in his chosen world, worked his way up to a deacon in his church (be prepared to be a deaconess). You'll recognize him. There's going to be a gold tooth hidden somewhere in his mouth. He may wear a gold chain (under his shirt and tie so that the minister, who probably wears one under his robe, will continue to think he's a pillow of the church). He doesn't wear the chain so much for manhood reasons; he likes to acquire things to symbolize his acquisitions. He's into things, video cameras, VCRs on all of his TV sets, at least one with a super screen, when everybody comes over for the Super Bowl. In the parking lot, he's got one of the biggest old-style Cadillacs, or maybe it's a Lincoln (if he owns a compact car, it's used as a gas-saver on weekdays, but not on Sundays.) Image is everything to this BMW, not to mention his lady. He's definitely into polyesters, especially pants that are too short.

A lot of your blue collar lover's days are spent in "uniform," so he doesn't bother to keep up with the subtle changes in men's suits. He likes to see his woman in fur stoles, but you can easily convince him that the other deacons' wives have gone to Burlington's Coat Factory and bought fur coats, he'll want you to be no less than them. In the summertime, he uses a camper, goes fishing with a neighbor or a coworker. He belongs to the Shriners and greatly admires the "Potentate" and secretly expects to fall heir to that throne. Or maybe he's a Mason or a member of a clandestine lodge with strict canons of behavior for continued membership. He may be balding, but refuses to part with or cut off the rest of his hair and may brush any available strands over his bald spot in a futile attempt to camouflage his balding. Or maybe he has a toupee. But most of the time, every Saturday, he's washing and polishing his car and manicuring his lawn while "my woman," as he calls her, is steaming and pressing her usher's uniform for Sunday, or cooking the Sunday dinner in advance so they can "come in eating," or cleaning the house, including the plastic-covered furniture in rooms that are seldom used but saved for any guests to see.

He's a great guy if you want someone who tends to be somewhat politically conservative, a moderate in matters of deportment, motherhood, apple pie and family values. His pride and joy is in his "home." After all, he's pulled himself up by the bootstraps, and wonders why the brothers he sees on the six o'clock news don't have any boots, aren't making it like he is. As for materialism, he pulls out all the stops for holidays and Christmas (he isn't yet into Kwanzaa). He often brags about his wife's cooking, as he pats his pudgy stomach and says "she knows how to make a man happy," forgetting his high blood pressure (about the only thing that could keep him from celebrating his golden (50th) wedding anniversary.)

This is a man who represents stability, longevity, and security. Unlike the professional man, he's able to hustle odd jobs on the side and part-time menial jobs. Because he's in the majority, sisters would do well to take full stock of the blue collar brother. If it's been your experience that professional men are threatened by you, this brother is likely to be proud and always bragging that his wife is a school teacher or a social worker, though he might not say it to you. Marriages of black professional women and blue collar men were frequent before the 1960s, in the days when many black men who had gone to college found jobs as policemen, mailcarriers, pullman porters, or whatever. They were pillows of the community.

So take a second look at the blue collar lover, the next time you're at the meat counter in the supermarket, or take your car to the shop, or forced to take public transportation, or attending the Shriners Ball, or asked to join a bowling league. You may be standing next to your BMW.

Will He Be A Self-Help Soulmate
Or A Corporate Climber?

You will keep running into these brothers. They're always building air castles and can talk for hours without end about what they're going to do. In fact, they talk so much about what they're going to do, they seldom seem to get around to doing it. Oh, they may enter a social program for small business development, and they're forever taking a course at the city community college or wherever they are found. They attend all the lectures pushing "self-help" among our people when civil rights and reform leaders are in town. And they wouldn't miss Tony Brown. But that's it.

In their defense, they'll tell you that it's hard to find a sister who wants to start a business with them or continue their jobs while they start it alone. They say black women don't have the patience, that they're too hooked on "the man" and his system of security. Some can go way down into the realm of sociobiology to explain this basic difference between the male and the female and trot out a limitless array of black intellectuals to explain the way it intertwines with all the elements of racial repression. They explain the psychohistory of why they think the African-American woman is not a self-starter. But, frankly, what it boils down to in the sister's mind is the difference between the self-employed and the employed male.

If your main concern is economic security, you are likely to go with the corporate type. Otherwise you may experience some trouble trying to distinguish between the brother who's truly trying to make it on his own, and might someday, as over against the brother who isn't really trying and, worse, may simply be playing the game. Seems like both are constantly borrowing from you at the end of the month (and periodically in between) to get them out of hock or help out in a feast-or-famine life that is generally more famine than feast.

Sisters in the latter category tend to keep an eye on the corporate brother, the one who has already made it, who has a proven job and security. However, some may set their standards too high, as a coterie of scholars suggested in an *Ebony* magazine article some years ago, "Do Black Women Set Their Standards Too High?" These sisters aren't settling for any middle managers. They want a brother who is in the Fortune 500 or The Black Enterprise 100. Never mind if none is there, she'll wait until he gets there.

Many times you'll find her sauntering through the financial district at noonday in any city, preferably the busiest corner, searching downtown lunchtime streets for a black man of high finance, usually in vain. She soon feels lucky just to bump into a black man walking by in a business suit and a brief case. There are men who have come to the attention of authorities for exploiting her desires, dressing up and initiating relationships with lonely corporate women or corporate-craving women and setting them up for "the Sweetheart Swindle."

For many sisters, when it comes to choosing a mate, if it isn't a matter of the luck of the draw, it's six in one hand and a half a dozen in the other. So let's begin to be more scrutinizing, regardless of your preference, starting with the self-help brother. They're cropping up everywhere, because of the current job shortage, but are a bit more likely to be found in the inner cities. A lot of black women who have lived on both coasts, and even in the Midwest, have said that the reason why many marriages hold together in the South, children and all, is because small towns and small communities have small churches and small social groups — what early sociologists called "primary groups," — those on the level of family and friends, or small enough for you to interact with on an individual basis, directly.

You get this testimony from black women all over the country, many who've live in both places, young and old. In small towns and small communities, where certain sanctions are usually present.

For instance, it's harder for a husband or a wife to carry on little dalliances and afternoon peccadilloes in smaller towns because everybody in town is aware of all the actions. In big coastal cities like New York and Los Angeles, the loneliness is in large part a product of anonymity and not being known, and you can be left alone and ignored a lot of the time whether you need to be or want to be or not. Flirtations, tippin' and dippin' and "hittin' on" the opposite sex for dates, furtive glances, come-hither grins, wicked winks, and slippin' and slidin' are more permissible under the cloak of anonymity and social isolation, where you can't hear about your friends except on the job and there's nobody to pull your coattail when you stray from the proper path.

This could be why many black women have found the smalltown Southern brother more to their overall satisfaction, a bit more domesticated than the black male who travels up and down the mean streets of inner cities, North and South. These days, according to the *The Wall Street Journal,* growing numbers of women, many of them black, are themselves forsaking the corporate world because they find it not to their liking due to family interests, the children or some other duality. However, the black woman is less privileged to leave the corporation for personal whims and, being a "twofer," may inadvertently collaborate with white women, Asians and other immigrants, to dampen corporate reception to the black male. On top of this, many black women are making bigger salaries now, and quite a few sisters are going to have to get used to out-earning her man, if she wants to have and keep a BMW, as he may have to be self-employed, due to the less amicable corporate environment and his special psychological reactions to this as an oppressed male.

Many sisters fail to see any differences between the black male and female in the way in which inability to thrive in the marketplace affects their psyches and their relationships with their soulmates and significant others. But, leaving that aside, if your BMW can't get into the corporation as readily, for whatever reason, you may have to reinforce, however cautiously, his incentive to self-employment, if he has it. At least the business or self-employment can provide compensatory status and a social front (even if it's literally a storefront) to hold off adverse outside criticism from your friends and relatives and in-laws as well as stimulating him. With your corporate salary and the tax you save from his losses, when allowable, you and your marriage may be able to make it to the other side of the hill or till times get better.

Remember, it's not always the best idea to sell the self-help brother short. John H. Johnson, founder of *Jet* and *Ebony* magazine and the entire Johnson Publishing Company empire, was a self-help type, never worked in a corporation but built his own from the $500 he borrowed from his mother who hocked her furniture, as I believe the story goes. That'd probably be equal to a good $5000 now. Nothing to play with, but you get the picture.

Not to set anybody up for the big rip-off, but we'll give a person our love, our hearts and our lives, but will hold them to every penny, when it comes to money, and won't take a chance on them like a mother might. A sister told me one night in Oklahoma City that the first things she wants to know when she meets a brother is if he has a negative HIV and a positive cash flow. You've heard it said that money marries money, but I can tell you that a lot of times poverty marries poverty.

You may have to make a choice, do you want a man or money, a man with money, or a man with or without money. I hear you. But, if money is everything to you, you may need to get ready to get it for yourself. This indeed is the plight of many sisters who have their condominium, a luxury automobile, and all the perks, but have to go without a man, in many cases resorting to what a Howard psychologist, Audrey Chapman, calls "mansharing." Prof. Chapman suggests the "a la carte" approach, where women use one man as an escort, one as a male friend or companion, another for sexual gratification and so on, choosing their men cafeteria style. But this is only if you can't find and keep a BMW and have given up hope, perhaps going into sexual anorexia, experimenting with celibacy or prepping for polygamy.

On the other hand, you may have found a very dedicated union of death-do-us-part monogamy with a brother who's never going to do anything, have anything, or go anywhere. He's just going to be piddling in his business and trying to produce or do wild or unusual things that you know will never work, because not everybody can come up with a pet rock or a hula hoop.

In any case, both of you shouldn't quit your jobs to go into business. In fact, it may not be a good idea for either of you to quit your job until the side business is making it well enough to demand it. Even a part-time job can help keep cash flow going, at least enough to scrape together the rent during inevitable cash flow squeezes and allow you to endure long enough to make the business work, which is often a minimum of three or four years, even when it works. It'll also lessen your anxiety, freeing up emotional energy and creativity for the business endeavors and keeping down a lot of bickering and battling back and forth between you and your mate as a by-product of frustations in finances and the business.

For that reason, it's always good to have a nest egg, perhaps a small savings earmarked for business use, as well as a steady source of money such as a pension, or stipend or some kind of part-time job, if not fulltime, when you're starting out in the early years. If, by contrast, you're making $100,000 a piece in the corporation, it's a good idea to have what European Jewish immigrants once called a "push cart" or some kind of small business on the side in case things go wrong for you in the corporation. Which is also a good reason to try to reinforce the business efforts of your mate. Furthermore, you may find that IBM for many means *"I Be Moved,"* so don't let the system catch you with your guards down.

Train What You Want

A mother's fondness for giving birth to sons instead of daughters is a strange reality splashed across newspapers and television screens in this country and elsewhere worldwide. So great is this tendency in parts of Asia (fueled by stringent population control measures) that, unlike black folks who have a man shortage, they face a woman shortage. Despite the fact that no penalties are imposed on births according to a baby's gender in America, many observers have noted an unspoken love for boys on the part of women, especially black women, to have and love boys in preference to girls.

To psychologists, this might point to repressed heterosexual impulses from mother to son in a world where black men are too often missing. Sociologists note that psychological and sociological decimation conspire to produce a black male shortage, which in turn seduces black women unconsciously to self-impose this preference for the male child in the bearing and rearing of children. Also, a girl requires a lot of attention to grooming and so on, but whatever the reasons — long before the song by a black male group, "I'll Always Love My Momma," hit the soul charts in the 1970s — people have accused black mothers of "raising their girls and loving their sons to death," or "spoiling them to death."

Suddenly single through divorce, separation or death, and finding themselves without a man, too many sister friends will make their young boy the "only man in my life" or "the man of the house" or "my little man." They shower the boy with unwanted attention and hugs and kisses, clothes and gifts like he is their pimp. Coming up in this circumstance, many boys get used to this relationship and "pimp" their mothers for the rest of their lives. Some move on to "pimp" their female lovers in adulthood, as well.

This practice has been thought to be a part of the motivation and making of the traditional street pimp. No less than Iceberg Slim for one has pointed to this childhood relationship with his mother as the source of his own psychological training ground for his own development as a pimp. Particularly when a boy is considered "cute" by European standards, the mother's girlfriends and other women are prone to chime in like one admiring chorus. "Ain't he cute," they marvel with no concern for his presence. "He's gonna be a heartbreaker — he's gonna be a ladykiller!" Too often this idle prophecy isn't lost on his future sexual endeavors, as more than quite a few may actually grow up to kill a mate.

I know a very conscientious black woman whose husband was one of the lesser known black militant activists in the late 1960s. After he fled to Cuba to avoid prosecution for a murder charge, she bravely proceeded to raise her two children, including a boy, alone. As part of her preparation of the boy for life, she would often say to him, "you don't have to take nothin' from no bitch." "I don't want none of these ho's and bitches messin' over my son," she once explained to her startled women friends, returning without skipping a beat to the clatter of complaints about the way black men were "messing over" black women, including herself.

In other ways, she frequently sought to mold her son in the fashion of her own ego ideal, hoping to approximate the qualities of the husband who had left her in many subtle ways, long before he hijacked the plane to Cuba. "You're a goodlooking young man," she would tell her young son over and over. "You'll be able to have any woman you want. So don't settle for no bear, no dog, no ugly black heifer. Make any of these women do what you want them to do for you. They can take care of you financially, emotionally and

114

physically. They ought to be happy to have somebody as young and fine as you on their flabby arms."

Psychologists have suggested that black women of this mind-set have internalized the negative feelings they complain about in their men and turned them into positives for the boys they are trying to mold into men. These women seek in their sons the man they have loved and lost. In the face of their own thwarted emotional needs, feeling abandoned, left, demoralized, they inadvertently impair their sons in the unconscious wish to reproduce a replica of their lost mate they can have and hold in a life of loneliness and abandonment.

So be careful, young sister, when you talk with your girlfriends, talking about "these no-good niggah mens." Your son is listening. Like a virus you can't feel until it turns into disease, your comments and thoughts may become cancerous and turn into psychological sores in his adulthood love relations. From where he knows not whence, but he will feel it to the bone.

Bit by bit, like daily psychic karate chops, your thoughts and admonitions are seeping into the intricate pathways of his brain, saturating it, like bytes of emotional data in an overloaded computer disk. All the games you played with the men in your life and they played on you, are now being implanted, indelibly, in the gullible brain of your black male son. Did you think he didn't see you slipping out of the window on a Saturday night? Did you think he didn't know you were lying about the balance in your checking account? He knows you have the rent money and remembers that you said you were going to tell your Sweetcakes you didn't have a dime. You didn't know he worried about your pending eviction all the while you laughed off the problem and pretended, said repeatedly — sometimes adopting the air of a boast — that your rent was paid-up for the next six months.

His status as your son makes him privy to the games you play day by day on the telephone — "tell him I'm not home." He knows that you (his first love object, the very first model he will have of a woman) frequently court and play around on more than one man and he sees them righteously mistreating you. He sees how you use sex as a weapon, witnesses your false but timely headaches. Did you know that he heard you tell Nadine that you weren't worried about times getting hard "cause I'll always have my pussy — my 'bank'?" He was checking you every time you spoke of your "bank" while pointing in the direction of your vagina. Do you remember all the times you were on the phone while he was playing with his toys with one ear alerted to your boisterous conversation?

Be careful how you vent your surplus rage on a boy who would love a black woman. When the boy does something that calls out in your mind the fact that he is the spitting image of his father, don't tell him for the hundredth time that "you're just like your no-good father." If he's just like his no-good father, then he's no-good too and might as well begin to act that way.

And check those magazines on your coffee table, the ones you put out there to impress your friends — *Cosmopolitan, Elle, Vanity Fair, Vogue, Ladies Home Journal, Architectural Digest, People* and *W.* Can't you see their covers are forever filled with blondes and brunettes? On rare occasions, they'll have a sister with European features and no darker than a brown paper bag. Your magazines are a subtle but hypnotic showcase in still life celebration of the vaunted beauty of the white woman. These motionless icons of white beauty perennially playback to the boy his fantasies and longings that he will have and hold to look for in a woman. They comprise the unerring prisms through which he can scope your own most secret aspirations. Against this backdrop of your material possessions, they spotlight the twisted notions of "beauty" you will never possess.

Someday, he too will go out into the world in search of hidden replicas of you in a woman. Wishing to please you, and driven by powerful unconscious wishes and unknown fantasies, he skips through the technicolored multitudes of Afro-American womanhood but, alas, brings home to you your own fantasy self, which you inadvertently presented to him — a white woman.

Sisters, your boy is watching you. He sees you when you leave for the beauty shoppe and come back with a dyed-blonde rinse, reinforcing in him the deepest way the secret feeling that if blondes have more fun, it is a blonde with which he too can have fun the most, the one who can make him whole. You have said to him by your own behavior that, if you could be white like the white woman, you too could be worthy of the love of the lost black man and the black man his mother lost, his father. In your toddler's mind, this translates as white, as the ideal prototype of a woman, the kind my mother wishes to be. If I can love and be loved by the white woman — my mother's ideal — I will be able to complete the love of my mother.

It's all right for now. Too late for sorrow. If this is something you will have to live with, consider that you may have brought it upon yourself. You helped to lay the groundwork. So, be careful, young sisters, in the way you raise your boys. Take special pains that you don't raise more heartaches for another generation of black women. Don't be like the sisters chided by Sharazad Ali in *The Blackman's Guide To Understanding Black Women*.

Nine times out of ten, pscychologists say, a boy who

experiences difficulties growing up in his relationship with his mother will live out these problems in his adulthood love life. A lot of the brothers, especially those whose fathers were absent or in the home but unavailable — whose mothers had to be both mother and father, had to be the one to extend the goodies and to whack the boy's hands out of the cookie jar — may grow up to see the women in their lives as extensions of their mothers, as "cupboards." The brother who has the cupboard syndrome is probably going to be dependent on you — he's looking for a black *woman* working. He may not be a pimp, but may act like he is.

That's one reason it's getting harder to get your boys out of the house than your girls. After high school, a lot of them won't go to college, won't get a job or even join the military. While you're at work during the day they're using your house for several things: a hotel or motel for the young ladies they bring over, they run up your utility bills because they cook and eat all day long, including the food you thought you had left for your dinner when you get home. Sometimes you'll go to use your phone and the phone is dead because he's called every girl he's met all over the country. He may leave home just before you get off from work, to give the impression he's been out jobhunting, but you can smell the eggs and bacon, the television is still hot, the towels are still wet in the bathroom, and you know he's gone over to his girlfriends, to pimp both you and his girlfriends.

In many cases, we let our sons stay in our homes, full-grown men not paying you, even when he has a job, spending everything on himself, every penny on his car and his clothes and sometimes his drugs, but doesn't want to give you a dime. Plus, he's actually in the way of your search for a BMW. There're plenty of responsible black men out there who will tell you that, when they come to a woman's house and see a lazy son sitting around doing nothing, pimping his mother, that the boy is frequently resentful, sees him as an intruder, a rival, who's likely to take away his sugar tit. It's an unspoken competition for the woman's affection and attentions. Sisters who've gone through this say you've got to move these young brothers out.

But if he hasn't been trained to be the kind of man you'd want, he's likely to move on to live off another black woman, or women, looking forward to "Mamas Day," the 1st of the month, when the welfare checks come in. I know that this practice is rooted in the welfare policy of kicking the man out of the house or supporting only the women and the children but not their man. I'm talking about men who themselves have exploited this situation. So when you get one check he's getting several, since he's likely to be working more than one woman. He's like a collection agency with several accounts to collect. If you're ever attracted to one of these brothers, you'll learn to recognize that his affection escalates the closer it gets to Mamas Day.

You're probably reading this and saying "this has nothing to do with me, because I'm not on welfare." Well, let me introduce you to the Sweetheart Swindler. Often this brother shows up for dinner, where you've furnished the steaks, the wine, and the brand-name liquors. He's selected you precisely because he sees that you can take care of your material needs, in fact may have enough extra to make his time worth while. He's likely to be as well educated as you, but has fallen into the passtime of exploiting the black male shortage.

He could be a bit younger. He's read the books and magazines and listened to the talk shows where women like you have said they don't want an old man, no dentures in the Efferdent, no walkers, no Ben Gay or Sloan's liniment smelling in the bathroom.

The Sweetheart Swindler may start by changing the oil in your car, especially if it's a nice car, he'll volunteer to take it to the service station. But while he's out, he'll take the opportunity to drive around and show-off to his friends. He'll do little things around the house for you, even light plumbing, many things your late husband or your ex may have been inclined to neglect. He cuts the grass, shampoos the carpet, washes the car, and sometimes will even do windows. He anticipates that he'll be rewarded — gifts become designer's suits, belts, shirts, Italian shoes. Holidays are coming up, and there are gatherings or places you'll want to go with him. Summer time is coming up and you plan to take him with you, so you'll rationalize getting him matched up and ready for the cruise.

Once your girlfriends see him, they'll fuel the fantasy with their talk about "Honey (or Sisterfriend), how did you get that fine thing that knows how to dress so well?" To this you put your hand on your hip and say, "Girl, I want a hero, not a zero."

Later, Prince Charming gets "a little short on the rent" or "Baby, I can't take you out to the club" (or to visit your grand-mother) "cause my car note is overdue." He's setting you up for the Sweetheart Swindle, when he'll borrow a few thousand dollars, then stage a fight to justify breaking up or simply disappear from sight.

The Sweetheart Swindler may be filling a need. I personally think it's sick, but I've heard sisters say "I hadn't laughed in fifteen years" until he came along, or I'm jogging again, or "Girl, I just joined the spa." Some say that "a young man a day keeps the doctor away." For a little while.

In the long run maybe we're going to have to teach our daughters to make better choices. Have her read Dr. Gwendolyn

Goldsby Grants, "The Best Kind of Loving."

Check Out the Nerd. Maybe some of you sisters should consider putting an end to your inclination to shun brothers who are nerds, Don't forget that nerds, or at least some of them, can be improved if they are cultivated. When young women students and postgraduates come up to me seeking advice on finding a mate or complaining that their man doesn't have the kind of chutzpah or verve they desire, I often tell them to "train what you want."

You can find a lot of nerds who can be turned into more than passable lovers if not charismatic personalities. Because of the problem of improprieties, I won't call the names of any outstanding or well known brothers who, in their early courting days, were truly nerds (I don't want to spoil any existing images or set myself up to get sued for telling too much of the truth). But let me tell you this, if you really want a BMW, you're more likely to find him in a nerd that wants to work than the hip hop dude per se or the already slickly polished brother.

Go out and find yourself a nerd, Sister. Know that you can be a little aggressive with the brother who is a nerd than you can or need to be with the come-on-let's-get-it-on type who comes on to everybody he bumps into, not just you. Maybe on your first day in college, or in the labor force, wherever, you should do a couple of things simultaneously. While you're identifying your courses and locating the classrooms, establishing yourself in the dorm, discovering the hippest hangouts, whatever, keep one eye open for any passing nerds. Chances are you'll be watching some future MVPS in the corporate world, the MD's, PhD's and LLD's who, in the winter of your later life together, can afford to supply your BBD's as well as a glorious fireplace in a charming country home and luscious snuggies to keep you warm. Start earmarking the nerds.

The 10 Cardinal No-No's

1. Running in Pairs, Or Three Is a Crowd. You'd think most sisters would know this but — if they do — they act like they don't. Number 1, never go to a party or a dance, a dinner or a house party, any social function, with more than one girlfriend. Certainly no more than one and a half of them. If you just must take another sister with you — and I mean if and only if you must — make certain she isn't knock-em-dead gorgeous, especially when you know you've let the hair "go home," let your extensions stay in too long, or you've been eating too many French fries to squeeze into the spandex pants because, after all, they'll only expand or stretch so far.

Failing that, try to take someone who's hopelessly in love with someone who would have been there with her himself except for his overtime work or travel schedule. In any case, find out what this sister plans to wear. You certainly don't want to look like gold dust twins and give a BMW the dithers trying to resolve the dilemma of which one he wants to choose.

My advice is to select a girlfriend who doesn't look nearly as good as you for your running buddy. If she's gregarious, polished, with a well-modulated voice, and plucks her eyebrows more often than somebody takes over the microphone or center stage from Patti LaBelle, leave her so-and-so at home and get yourself some kind of alternate.

Finally, even if the band plays your favorite song, with no man coming up to ask you to dance, never, ever dance with your girlfriend, even if you don't live in San Francisco. There's always another song and another dance. And you never know if a BMW was just then trying to get his courage up to start an a capella conversation that might have led to wedding bells and "Here Comes the Bride."

2. Bushwhacked and Sidetracked by the Married Brother. If you should ever find yourself attracted to a married brother, maybe you should run, as fast as you can. Just pretend you're Flo Jo after that gold — I mean the medal, except you'd better be running away from the medal because even if you did catch it, it would most likely turn out to be a chain around your neck, an albatross.

Don't believe everything you hear or that your BMW tells you. People really don't change their habits. So, even if you manage to move another sister out in the cold, don't be surprised when it turns around and happens to you. I once had a client who was dating a married man and, happily for her, she became one of the exceptions: he actually married her after divorcing his wife. But hold on, the plot thickens. She settled with him into a storybook home life after a fabulous wedding and honeymoon to match. Both got mentioned, believe it or not, in national magazines and major dailies of their respective home towns. Then came the winter of his discontent, except that it arrived in the middle of summer. Her dream man, returning to his old pursuits, took to staying out every weekend with someone else. When she questioned him, he reminded her that, "you knew I played when *you* were seeing me."

His frank admission was anti-climactic, as she'd already seen them together, knowing the places where she used to go with him when he was married to somebody else. I guess it's reasonable to expect that what goes around comes around, even if it's you. The moral is you can't pat a snake on the head and think you suddenly have a house pet that won't bite you. If you play you must pay.

3. Never Name the Most Expensive Restaurants,or Clubs, Theaters or 5 Star Hotels Until *After* **the First Four Dates.** On the other hand, don't name a Motel 6 or any third rate hotel either. Your potential BMW might get suspicious of a low rent rendezvous. Either way, it's likely to be a real turnoff. Besides, he'll quickly see through you. People can generally tell what you're used to. Especially is this true of persons who are always boasting of going first class as you observe them in their polyester from head to toe.

On the early dates you're trying to get into the brother's head and it's mainly a matter of emotions. You want a restaurant on a first date to have a certain charm and sophistication, so you might suggest the little neighborhood deli or mom-and-pop around the corner.

It might be a good idea to eat before you go because, once there you'll want to remember to order something light, a Caesar salad or soup or soup and salad. It'll help you to eat with easy finesse while leaving you free to concentrate on him and the conversation. He doesn't get the impression that you're going to be competing with his mortgage every time he takes you out. You don't want to give the brother an excuse to start suggesting going Dutch. Keep him in the African tradition of paying for his woman.

After about the fourth date, if you think you've won his heart, or at least his confidence, you can move into a little more upscale restaurant. Even then, avoid ordering anything with bones and barbecue or a cream sauce, where you have to use a box of napkins or wish you had a bib. Save that for the time he's going to take you down to Texas for his high school or family reunion, where he may prefer you to appear at home and somewhat regular. You simply don't have time for cracking crabs, dipping from sauce to sauce or any serious eating at this point. You don't want to turn him off before you can get him under your spell.

4. Don't Get The Horse Before The Cart. Don't care how fine or pretty this brother might be, never, never have sex with him on the first three dates (never mind that he may bolt after the second date). It's not just that you haven't known him long enough to even know his views on HIV testing and STD (socially transmitted diseases). He might say, "oh, that's only for gays and bisexuals and drug addicts. He could be all three — you wouldn't know after a couple of dates.

Unfortunately, on a romantic level, most men don't believe they're really that special. They'll conclude instead that what you do with them, or for them, you must have done, or soon will, with all the others. Most men are dying to get in bed with you anyway and Heaven help you if you permit this before the chemistry is there. It's like when you turn on your favorite soap opera, you can tell if the romantic lead has been thrown into a sexual encounter before the romantic chemistry is established.

Even if it doesn't turn him off, you might wind-up a sexual casualty, caught up in a sexual liaison with a person with whom there's no way you can get along. Day after day, you'll wait in vain for your phone to ring, hurrying home to play back your phone messages, only to find that his voice isn't on the tape. If you're bold enough to call him, you only get his message tape and its excerpt from Luther Vandross. Your phone may never ring again. You can call and call but you will never hear from him. Then you're off to the shrink.

If you study the animal kingdom, you will see that the male is intrigued, enthralled, with the sexual chase. Maybe the pursuit is to the male what foreplay is to the woman. If you are an aggressive feminist and desire to reverse the rules of Mother Nature by inviting him to bed, rest assured that he will accept your invitation but not necessarily your inclination. You'll run into no sexism here, no opposition to role reversal. He'll be glad to leave you flat of your back to get his feet back in the streets.

Although you were never placed on the pedestal by the white man or the ways of the white world, the black man wants to put you on his pedestal in his own personal way, wants you at least to be his "queen". So you must carry yourself with royalty.

I know there're sisters who, as feminists, will say they don't want to be on a pedestal, wouldn't want to be a queen. Just tell them to get out of the way of the sisters who can appreciate it, after so many centuries of standing by while the white women sat perched on the pedestal. Make way for sisters who are able to rejoice that they can finally get a chance to know how it feels to be elevated above the realm of the underclass, barely making ends meet, being called bitches and ho's while enduring the daily hardships of material and emotional sacrifice, doing with out. Then to be plucked and lifted from this crushing existence to the comfort of the high class to the lofty ambience of mint julep, enjoying our own maids, housekeepers, and daylong ease, with a healthy expense account to boot, is something to be desired. But not by the "queens" of a people whose royalty continues to be denied.

5. When and Where You Enter or the Setup for Date Rape. Never let any of the first five dates take place at your man's pad or pied-a-terre, whether he lives there or not, because he may be married and using a male apartment pool for his outside sexual plunder, something like the character in the award-winning movie, *The Apartment.*

126

Don't forget that the jury is still out on the date rape situation. This brand-new social malady isn't confined to the white co-educational campus anymore than AIDS is to the white gay closet, where it began. Maybe you aren't appalled that Mike Tyson, the people's heavyweight champion of the world, is locked away in an Indiana prison because a Sunday school teacher beauty contestant went up to his motel room in the wee-wee hours of the morning to continue a conversation about going out to take some pictures.

There's no excuse for rape, but precisely because you will be alone in the room with him, you put yourself or/and your potential BMW unnecessarily at risk, resting your case on which one of you a jury happens to believe. But, as Desiree Washington Mike Tyson's accuser, has discovered, you and your slick white prosecutor can convince a white jury without fooling the general public. Stay out of the brother's room unless you already have your hooks in him or know you can handle any situation that might arise.

I said the first five dates, because — especially, if you're not at your own place, you need enough time to get familiar with the terrain, if not the brother. You need to have your whistles ready, your mace, alarms, and know how to find the rolling pin. At least the fly swatter. You should have your hat pin with you, or something, in case you need a way to get the brother's attention.

So if you don't mind somebody seeing you, the advantage is in yor own pad. You could also let some neighbor know he's coming up (some neighbor is likely to be snooping or peeping anyway). They're already familiar with your modus operandi, and would be alert to any new gentleman or unusual noises coming from your place. You know how to signal them, if necessary, the nearest walls, what doors will open, what exits, secret tunnels, what windows will let up, the sliding doors, the fire escapes, in case things get too raunchy. You know about all the telephone extensions.

Incidentally, if you're living alone and playing in the BMW market, maybe you ought to install a telephone in your bedroom closet. This is your secret backup communications piece to 911, a neighbor or security. Have the emergency numbers programmed into automatic dialing. You don't want to be shelved into a closet and left there for the cleaning lady to discover. You never know when Mr. Hyde may turn into Dr. Jekyll, and according to Dr. Morris Jeff, a leader of black social workers, if the argument takes place in the bedroom, the victim is more likely to be the woman; in the kitchen, it's more likely to be the man. You figure it out, but in the interim, if you don't want to get your powder wet, don't go near the water.

6. Knowing Your Past Could Set You Free. Never fail to do some probing, some sniffing around your potential BMW's past relations. This might take the form of a simple "hint" to others who have known him, or you could come right out and ask about his previous escapades and disappointments. This is an ancient cardinal principle that may be obvious to some of you, but it is puzzling to many others who pride themselves on not being "nosy."

You need to know how your future BMW treated the *women* in his family and how they treated him, whether he's gone through the necessary stages of psychological and social development. Not that you couldn't salvage him in spite of all, but you'll need to know its effect on him before you can hope to do any damage control. You should find out what he's doing about it, and so on, if you want to make a useful assessment of what you're getting yourself into.

Too often, we women marry our fathers, so to speak, and fight out unresolved conflicts with our mates (who are extensions of our fathers). When men do this, in connection to their mothers, psychologists call it the "cupboard syndrome." In women we might call it the "knight's armor complex." Once married, we are prone to fight out our sibling rivalries with our mates, if only because it was with our fathers or father substitutes that we first learned how to love, hate and deal with interpersonal relationships in our families, especially with members of the opposite sex.

Sometimes the choice of a mate as psychological ego representations in the image of our fathers turns out to be a very good match, especially if the image of our fathers and the relationships with our brothers were not discouraged during the days of our youth. But a lot of women seek out men who remind them of the "bad character types" in men they grew up around and in their lives within the inner city, especially the so-called underclass. These may often have been negative, restricted and distorted, to paraphrase the late psychologist Amos Wilson in *The Psychological Development of The Black Child*.

Then, when things don't work out on a personal level, we too often displace our rage or sublimate it in compensatory social reactions such as zealous commitment to anti-male and anti-family feminism, because we didn't get our infantile baggage organized and packed away before embarking on our relationships. Consequently as black women we harbor an awful lot of unresolved conflicts — from fathers who deserted our families or didn't treat our mothers right, manytimes some woman we knew in our extended family or circle of acquaintances or friends growing up, not to mention the men who've done us wrong. So, to get the baggage straight before embarking on a sexual romantic journey makes all good common sense.

In countries with bonafide aristocracies or simple monarchies, serious tests are often given both parties to a marriage, to prevent any unanticipated medical histories and histories of mental illness and social instability. Some even probe the longevity of the family or parental authority, not to mention the lineage problem. Within the middle class today, there're even people who slip into alcohol and drug abuse, knowing that sometimes the curse is visited upon the third generation.

Remember, it's easy to get into a hope-to-die kind of love with a man who's just not for you precisely because of such unconscious strivings and unfulfilled psychological needs and compensations. You're suddenly fighting with your man and don't know why. It doesn't help to rationalize this situation with such sayings as "you know, opposites attract."

7. Never, Never Continue to Make all the Telephone Calls Hunting Him Down Like You're the IRS. What if he doesn't call? It's been three days since he promised to. Should you call him? What if he never calls you? You wonder if maybe just that one call could have made all the difference — maybe you'd be living now in the little white house with a picket fence or whatever.

You've heard it passed on — "never be available." Don't call him." Too available? How are you going to get to know him? I do think I should give a word of caution about the the early stages of a new relationship. Hold up at any stage if you find you're doing almost all of the calling and getting only his answering machine with Anita Baker or whatever husky voice of the moment he might be into when you call. Be careful until you get to know the man because getting to know him allows you to learn to know just how far you can go in playing this controversial strategy by ear.

In the early 1980s, when we were running Kupenda (Swahili

for ''to love'') or Black Love Groups, the question of whether a woman should phone a man came up, and after about an hours deliberation, the men and the women came to a consensual agreement that it's okay for a woman to call a man but not more than he calls her. Of course, as I said, this is in the early stages. Once you have a serious thing going on, you'll be much freer to do what you feel like doing. It's just like fishing, you can do things once the fish has bitten the bait which you'd better not do before.

On the other hand, beware of the brother who wants your phone number but won't give you his. This is usually a dead give away that he's either married, has a roommate somewhere, or is into something serious one way or another. This makes it a good idea to get his phone number, but you don't have to wear it out just because you have it. But don't forget to dial the number at least once just to check whether the number is his or even exists.

Some people will advise you to pretend not to be at home or available sometimes, even when he calls you. But I know a couple including a brother who was a political activist imprisoned for about five years at the end of the Black Power Movement in the late 1960s and early 1970s. To this day, he showers praise and appreciation on his mate recalling that not a day passed while he was in prison that he didn't call her at least once and that he never once, in five years, called her and she didn't answer or wasn't there. Today, she's still his wife and soulmate to boot.

A lot of brothers — and sisters too — have a way of calling to check if their sweet thing is still at home. But now you have the Star 65 system on the telephone for about five dollars a month. It'll let you know who it was that called you and hung up. It'll also allow you to keep tabs of your BMW's true whereabouts when he calls, if you need to know. I know you're normally not a snooper, not normally anyway, but you never know when something might come in handy. Normally, it does, though you can overdo anything, even too much of a good thing is bad.

8.   Never Go into Combat Without "Protection." We're living in the days of AIDS and God knows what else next. So you'd be foolish to engage in sex without a condom. Not that condoms will protect you 100 percent if you choose the wrong "man," but neither would a bulletproof vest protect you from a pistol in every single case. This has nothing to do with the exploitation of AIDS and condoms by Planned Parenthood and their governmental collaborators in the genocidal efforts to control black births. We'll take care of that in another way. We have to learn to pick our battles, when and how to fight, and how to be selective in the sack. Anybody you decide to have a child with should already be a certified BMW and you'd be fairly certain you're not facing too many risks, because you'd already be on your way to the altar, if you haven't already tied the knot. We're talking about an individual matter here.

It's amazing to hear these days, in any case, that school teachers have to tell black kids to wear a condom. In the days before the pill and abortion on demand, just about everybody wore condoms all the time, and boys carried them in their wallets even though most weren't getting any chance to use them in those days. If you didn't have a condom to put on wasn't nothing going on. In the words of a contemporary song: "ain't nothing shaking but the leaves on the trees, and they wouldn't be shaking if it wasn't for the breeze."

If you had so much as mentioned a condom to the teacher, the entire school, let along the classroom, would have come to a screeching halt, screeching from your backside sliding down the hallway corridor to the principal's office where your parents would be waiting or on the way. It worked.

So tell your junior Magic Johnson to come up with a condom or come back another day. Would you hit the highway on a motorcycle without a helmet? Walk into a boxing ring without a mouthpiece? Fence without a mask? Probably not. Same thing. Sex may not be violent, but it can still be deadly, and the life you save may be your own. If he cares about you, he'll go along with the program. Good riddance, if he doesn't. Tell the brother to get to skipping. You'll save yourself a lot of trouble without a doubt. If you really want a BMW and don't mind waiting for the real thing, here's a non-negotiable motto: "no condom, no sex."

Otherwise if you don't protect yourself, you can't blame anybody else. We were amazed a few years ago when black leaders of social service and civil rights organizations started pushing something called "male responsibility" to teenage blacks. They found out that if there's going to be responsibility in adolescent sexual matters, it'll generally be exercised by the female, if being responsible means resisting sex. In the overwhelming majority of cases I've observed, if the young woman will, the young man will. Who has the most to lose? Who's at the greatest risk of illegitimate pregnancy and AIDS from unprotected heterosex? If that isn't enough to coax responsibility, what can you expect from the risk free male, not to mention the undeniable differences in the sexuality of males and females.

For decades until our time, males exercised responsibility for one simple reason, called a shotgun, as in "shotgun marriage." A young fellow either kept "a condom on his johnson or his ass in a sling." Otherwise young sisterfriends, it's simple: "you fuck, don't pass the buck." Even a prostitute demands her money up front, these days, a condom *and* the money. Motto: "don't be no 'ho where there ain't no dough." Got to fight the power.

9. Never brag about your corporate perks and your credit cards. Heard about the "Sweetheart Swindle?" You should see victims in the clinical office. Seems there're brothers out there (buppies, Black Urban Professionals) in the exclusive upper middle class suites exploiting the black male shortage in the upper echelons, converging on beaches and other romantic places such as Nassau, Jamaica, Hawaii, Tahiti and the Fuji Islands, picking up lonely black corporate females vacationing at corporate expense. The brothers are very adept at sweeping a sister off her feet. Some quickly move in on unsuspecting sisters with a promise to marry. Back home at last and courting from a distance (of necessity, as many are already married), the sweetheart swindler hits the swooning young woman up for a sizable loan or whatever before moving quickly out of her life, disappearing from sight forever.

So learn how to keep your possessions, if not your passions, to yourself. And don't start popping off about your fur coats, your district manager's position, your hefty expense account, your gold credit cards, your diamond rings, the luxury car your company changes every year. Before you know it, somebody else will be driving your car.

Watch taking the brother to lunch at all the fancy places too quickly, slapping down your gold credit card or the kind that must be paid in thirty days while positioning your wallet to flash the rest. The brother's brain cells will start to clicking and churning like a cash register. Watch yourself when he comes to your place and you ask him his preference for a drink and he wants brand name liquors, no generic brands, no scotch, just Chevis Regal, but always settles for the house brand in wines when you're out with him for dinner.

One corporate sister I know bought a Gucci belt from Neiman Marcus for her new beau for Christmas. She expected the brother, a hotel doorman, would well appreciate it, but he was really pushed out of shape when he found he'd only gotten a belt. The brother got an attitude and acted like he wanted to take the belt and use it on her. She might have heeded her warning signs before she presented the belt, when she prepared a brunch with eggs benedict. He thought the eggs were improperly cooked and said he'd never seen any eggs in all that mustard. Besides he said, he'd seen a belt he liked a whole lot better down at Sears and suggested he might trade it in. "What was that store you said you got this from?"

A good friend recently met what she thought was *the* man. She'd already been divorced for about ten years and had sworn off black men for the usual reasons, you name them. She'd gone on about her life, was working everyday and buying a small house, just taking care of herself, but she happened into her regular nail shop one day when a brother was there getting his nails done, and a pedicure. I believe he even asked the manicurist whether there was a place nearby where he could get a "decent" massage. He was a masculine-looking brother, a Roger Craig type, a younger version of Jim Brown combined with Muhammad Ali in his prime. She noticed how friendly the brother was. He was talking to her and all the women in the shop, very gregarious, an award-winning personality.

The second time she saw him was the day she happened into the shop as he was coming through the door. They fell in conversation and quickly exchanged phone numbers while her fingernails (and his toenails) were drying. They found they had a lot of things in common. He was divorced, he indicated, had the deeds to two or three houses he was thinking of putting on the market. He said he'd managed several car rental places and could rent a car anytime he wanted without showing anything, and just generally bragged about his social station in life.

When he finished first and left, it provided her the chance to ask the women in the shop about him. Everybody spoke highly of him, thought he was good as gold, said he'd been coming in there for maybe five years. They praised him very highly, said they thought the world of him, telling how he'd bring in champagne on special occasions and periodically a rose for the ladies.

While the story was being related to me, I was surprised that a sister wouldn't know in this day and age that any man who goes to a nail shop on a regular basis to get not only a manicure but a pedicure as well is either completely smitten with himself, gay, an entertainer, a hustler, a dope dealer, a con artist or pimp. Turns out this brother was almost all of the above. A brother like this may seem like a BMW, but he'll end up with *you* working — for him.

Somehow, despite all this, the sister in question did enter into an incredible picture-book whirlwind marriage. They married in two or three months — not enough time to find out if the brother had a weak bladder. Meanwhile, he convinced her it was wise for him to move in with her while he sought to place his houses on the market, saying he was temporarily in a "condo" which she later learned was the apartment of a vacationing friend. But he even showed her phony deeds to the house.

One day, as they were getting ready to go on a weekend drive, he asked her mother if he could use her credit card to rent a car to go down South and look at some property, because his "main man" was out of town or out of joint with his car but that the following weekend he'd have everything all straight. The brother had no deeds, no properties, no condo, let alone rental properties, no car, no credit cards and no credit. All he had was a silver tongue.

This is why a lot of sisters follow a low-key strategy of

downplaying their material worth, acting like they don't have a dime and the utility company is about to shut off their lights. To every hard luck story he creates, be ready to let him know the wolf is also knocking at your door. Unfortunately, when you try to impress a lot of brothers, you're more likely to impress the brother with nothing going for himself rather than one who's looking for something to hitch his wagon to.

Many brothers are actually turned off by your name-dropping about the big shot men or celebrities you've dated in the past or how wonderful or for that matter how bad earlier beaux were in comparison to your present heart throb. He'll never forget what you tell him either, even if he's the kind of man that can't remember where he left his hat last night. Besides he's likely to bring it back up to haunt you later on. Also, you can't necessarily keep a hope chest in the second marriage as you did in your first, the little keep-sakes of things you'd done together and whatever sentimental artifacts, letters and pictures, you kept in your drawer under the panties, thinking there will be no reason for the man to ever delve into your drawers.

This is the same as bringing up emotional baggage from the past, in a disagreement with your mate, like failing to wipe the slate clean and fighting out with him the things some previous man or men have done to you or somebody close to you: "I decided I was never in my life going to ever let a nigger do this to me, not to mention that" or "you thought I had forgotten what you did in 1942." The confessional is nothing but an unwanted retrieval from the hope chest of your mind. Remember hope more properly looks ahead, while hopelessness is tantamount to total defeat. What looks to the past is regret instead of hope. This brings us to another no-no.

10. Avoid Confessionals Altogether. Let this be your mot to: don't do anything you wouldn't want to see on television, because, believe it or not, you might. Even if you don't reach television or courtroom infamy, the confessional is your own personal broadcasting medium. When your mate is troubled, not to mention when your relationship is altogether broken, he's likely to tell it to a friend of his/or and your own, or tell it to some member of your family or your in-laws, who'll tell it to somebody close to them and so on till it reaches those who feed the grist to the rumor mill.

By merely confessing to your mate, you've planted it in the dark recesses of his memory data bank, to lurk there until someday he thinks he needs it. But, as I was saying, never do anything you wouldn't want to see on television. But if for any reason — Heaven forbid — you should do anything unsavory in the dark or otherwise, when light turns to day as it is likely to, even in Alaska, keep it to yourself.

I will never forget the couple that came in to marital therapy, he of high professional stature and she of a prominent family background. They were trying to patch things up after an eight months separation. One afternoon in the middle of the session, she sought to whip him over the head by telling of a Prince Charming she'd met on the jogging trail.

"I'll bet you had sex with him," he inquired.

"Yes," she quickly confessed before the therapist could interfere. Attempting to recover, the therapist suggested, "you mean during the time that you and your husband were separated."

"No, before *and* after."

As the therapist reeled momentarily, the angry husband bolted out of the door, never to return, leaving three children in a broken home.

Once again, confess only to the priest or the shrink or the lawyer, if it comes to that. These days, when shrinks talk and lawyers make deals and priests, not to mention preachers, who moreover are losing a lot of their contact with God, the jury isn't even in on telling anybody.

While we're at it, you might slacken up your enthusiasm for uncovering the shady, villainous transgressions of your mate from the past. You might not always be able to handle what you uncover.

Calling All Black Men

Calling All Black Men
Come out the closet!
Mr. Black Xerox-Clorox-
Mason-Christian-Muslim-
Democrat-Communist-Pan-
African-Wino-Dope smoker-
Coke Sniffer-Free baser,
Calling all Black Men
Mr. Black wife beater-
raper-robber-murderer-
worker-father-husband-lover
COME OUT THE CLOSET
Mr. Black Back-to-Africa
Mr. Black I-love-America
CALLING ALL BLACK MEN

© *By Marvin X*
San Francisco

A BMW Has His Say

by my BMW, Nathan

I could tell you about a whole lot of things, but I can't tell you why a black woman would get so fired up with the idea of a BMW, when she, herself, is already married to a vintage Rolls Royce. Maybe I ought to feel gratified that a lady Mercedes, who sometimes acts like a Lambourghini — especially considering that she's my wife and knows me better than anybody else — still thinks I'm a BMW.

Maybe a woman feels guilty enough already when she's hording a whole black man all by herself, let alone a BMW, something on a deeper level she may long somehow to share.

Who am I to say? I can testify, certainly, that Julia knows and practices the subject matter of her saucy little book. This lady has got to be, beyond a shadow of a doubt, the world's best mate selector.

Besides, we brothers are going to have to learn to listen when our women want to speak to us. Especially about this "man/woman thang." God knows black women have suffered in a world the white man rules. Black women will tell you: if black men could deal more effectively with the white man, black women could handle the white woman.

But the black male — from top to bottom too readily allowing himself to be misled — seems in some way or another bent on continuing to fail his role; so the black woman's been forced too often, over the centuries of our captivity, to live without the natural protection a woman needs from a man, including protection from the socioeconomic bear. Yet she's stuck by us to the bitter end, for the most part, through thick and thin, with sometimes hardly any clear reward, emotional or otherwise.

I remember a wall-high painting of a black woman I have twice seen hanging silently, tightlipped, in the Black Cultural Center at the University of Washington, under which the caption reads only: "Bearer of Pain" — referring, I suppose, to the many historical hurts the black woman's had to endure, from white *and* black men, relentlessly handed down the crooked corridors of our lost generations of enslavement, traumatizing the black woman's feminine mystique through the heartbreaking cacophony of intemperate tears and testimony and angry admonitions from her mother and her grandmother and other one-sided complaints overheard from the women who sometimes gossip about other women and "these no good nigger mens" — inadvertently reinforcing white society's cunning concoction of customs, laws, brainwashing and propaganda.

When I interviewed a representative sample of so-called strong black women for my second Ph.D. dissertation, on "Black Male/Female Relations" (I would later switch to "relationships") in the early 1970s, I found that they were prone to be very proud of their strength as a racial gender but felt that it was something forced upon them by unwanted circumstance, and they were afraid this very strength would someday be the death of them in their relationships with their mates. Most said they would give their right arm to have a strong black man to stand beside them but, under the socioeconomic constraints in which the black race finds itself, that is a possibility that is closing down. Many frankly acknowledged that, if they could find a good man who would stick by them, who could take care of them and would, they'd give it all up for the man.

I also encountered many black men in my research activities

142

who readily conceded the black woman's historical role as the backbone of the black family, which she has held together in mean, disjointed times, of necessity, trying to be both mother and father to her children. I detected that many black men themselves secretly look up to the black woman, but resent it, don't know how to deal with the kind of woman the black woman tends to be.

The men I questioned had frequently grown up either without fathers present at all or with fathers who were there but generally unavailable to them. And so, as boys they had assimilated naturally enough to the feminine ways of coping they had learned from their mothers. As men they stand behind a macho veneer, reacting to real or imagined difficulties with passive aggression and unwanted dependency unbecoming to a man, and they often mask their chronic depression with cavalier posturing and mock hostility. Never having been taught the rudiments of male/female relationships in early childhood, they are much too ready to resort to violence and otherwise hard to live with, because they know no other way of standing up to a woman.

Growing up in a matrifocal condition, they hear their mothers say harsh and bitter things about their absent or wayward fathers, saying "yo pappy sho was a no good so-and-so." Then, whenever they display some variety of mischief disturbing to their mothers, they are told that they're going to be no good just like their no-good fathers, an admonition which helps to spur too many boys to accept the mantle passed down from their fathers and to commit themselves to acting that way, unequivocally.

Young girls witnessing this scenario, and manytimes watching their mothers being routinely fought or otherwise mistreated by their men, will tend to develop and harbor deep feelings of sexual ambivalence and antipathy. As grownup women, many will have intractable difficulty relating to a man. Either too ready to bristle or explode in volatile hostility on the one hand, or over-indulgent on the other, or both, they cling to a tightrope of anxious ambiguity in their desire to please a man for fear they won't be able to keep him.

I also noticed that, while black men see their problem as "the system," black women tend to see their major problem in life to be the black man. Middle class women appear to believe outright and furthermore that black men as a group use racism as an excuse in a spineless search for refuge from a debilitating socioeconomic plight. In the black man's mind, these women have inadvertently sided with the system. And so, black men and women, black couples, fight and contend and squabble with each other in angry fits and acrid bouts of misplaced rage they wish they could inflict upon an offensive system or their grievous personal situation.

I have watched them in the clinical office as well as in daily life, in both private and public settings, and I have coupled my observations with all the black woman talk about black male in-adequacy juxtaposed against the myth of the strong black woman. I concluded, nevertheless, that what we need is not fewer strong black women but more strong black men.

Before the rise of the white unisexual feminist movement and its seemingly unconscious, but perhaps inherent, antagonism to the black male, I could see that something special needed to be done by black men to restore themselves as a group to a position of respect and to get them back on the track in their natural role as men, something I heard Mr. Muhammad say in the old Chicago Armory when I was a graduate student at the University of Chicago.

A few years later, as a young sociology instructor at Howard University. I wrote an article, ''The Frustrated Masculinity of the

Negro Male,'' and sent it to the *Negro Digest,* then published by the Johnson Publishing Company. In the article, which appeared in the spring of 1964, I sifted through the many difficulties the African-American male experiences in his masculine role and ended with a quote from my now late friend, John O. Killens, in his novel, *And Then We Heard the Thunder,* where he had a woman character tell the hero, Solly: "The one thing they will not stand for is for a black man to be a man."

Hoyt Fuller, the editor of *Negro Digest,* wrote in his "Notes" in a subsequent issue that that article had elicited more letters than any the magazine had ever published — but all the letters had been negative, saying the black male wasn't frustrated, an intellectual stance which in the ensuing years would become full-blown in the form of "strong black family" overreactions to the so-called "Moynihan Report," which in 1965 suggested that racism had achieved the "terrible thing" of handicapping the black male's ability to make it in the marketplace, which in turn was crippling his ability to hold his family together. Moynihan called for a National Plan of Action, to include the mass employment of black males. After black intellectuals hit the ceiling, 70 per cent of more than twenty million new jobs created in the next fifteen years were given to women, most of them married, middle class and white.

Although black male intellectuals and leaders from the black bourgeoisie also immediately rolled their eyes over Moynihan's use of the great black sociologist E. Franklin Frazier's simplistic metaphor, "matriarchy," to describe the broken patriarchy of the African-American, these same intellectuals today are proclaiming, without any evidence that stands up under scrutiny and scholarly skepticism, that Africans had matriarchies in ancient Egypt and in overall African antiquity.

Yet, the national sample of 1,000 black women to which Julia and I distributed questionnaires in late 1969 did not see the white feminist agenda as amenable to the needs or interests of the black woman or the race. They said their circumstances and experiences and, therefore, their solutions are different and, when all is said and done, "there can be no freedom for the black woman without freedom for the black man,"

By contrast, black male intellectuals are fast becoming advocates of the white feminist agenda — without adding one idea or thought to it. Some think they're into something new by calling themselves "womanists" instead of "feminists." Either they were right in 1969 and wrong now — in case why change? — or wrong in 1969 and right now — which means at best that it takes them a long time to catch on.

As I have said elsewhere many times before but must say it again, our situation is this: the white woman has a hold to the white man's shirttail, holding on with all her heart, though screaming all the while. The black woman has a hold to the white woman's skirttail. And the black man has a hold to the black woman's skirttail, with the white man leading them all around like a conga dance.

In 1969, when Betty Friedan stood and said that "the blacks had the 1960s; women [meaning white women primarily] would have the 1970s," I began to say "don't forget the black male" — though it was no longer possible to be heard. I nevertheless did what I could.

Seeing a growing rift between black males and females (on top of anticipating that the black race would be worse off by the mid-1980s, because of the white race's genocidal reproductive agenda and its flagship feminist movement's disdain and discomfiture, if not inherent, outright antagonism to black male liberation), I determined to do all I could to foment a black male/female relationships movement, as a double-edged device for getting black people to see the political nature of the emerging black family problem their intellectuals and leaders were so vigorously denying in a blind abhorrence of any recognition of black family "pathology" — even as a consequence of oppression — in a mindless quest for racial acceptance, giving up our blues, our thunder, and the blitzing flashes of "Black Power."

As things rocked on, and the black movement took on an other-worldly Pan-African cast and began to slip back, while the white woman, aided and orchestrated by the white man, stole our blues and our thunder, I wrote an editorial, "Will the Real Black Man Please Stand Up?" in the May, 1971 issue of *The Black Scholar*, of which I was then founding publisher. I ended by saying

"There are only two kinds of black men — the broken who fall and the true black man who may have stumbled in the past but will rise again.

We as black men are breaking loose, with each passing day, from the shackles that bind us, both physical and mental, and becoming once again the real black man in the full tradition of our pre-European forebears.

We are rising and we will win. Victory is ours to seize, if we will but stand and seize it.

Will the real black man please stand up?"

The years passed quickly, while the black race fell into a comatose sleep, from which it has not awakened till this day. By 1979, within the ashes of the black consciousness movement, Julia and I had begun to put out a periodical called *Black Male/Female Relationships*. In the very first edition, under a banner headline, "Why Don't Black Men Organize As Men?" I called attention to a new organization of black men in the Midwest, The Knights in Shining Black Armor, which had formed to encourage the black male to "take a good look at yourself" and rally to the notion that "it's getting up time."

Some months later, I was asked to join the Steering Committee forming "The First National Conference of Black Men." Despite harsh opposition from feminist elements — and a media blackout/whiteout — one thousand black men gathered in the Oakland Arena by nine o'clock a.m. on a hazy Saturday morning in the late fall of 1980 and didn't disband all told until almost midnight. However, aside from intimidation for its militancy by the powers-that-be, employers and politicians, the group disagreed too bitterly over goals and direction and died.

Meanwhile, despite all the hue and cry in recent years about the "endangered black male," and "mentoring" tied to rites of passage programs (*Bringing the Black Boy to Manhood,* 1985) only two national black male groups have been established.

One of them, calling itself the "First National Association of African-American Males," first surfaced in Kansas City, where its keynote speaker (a career federal government bureaucrat appointed by Richard Nixon) literally broke down and cried during his speech when telling of his ex-wife's suicide and the pain that he, a black man of some national prominence, had had to bear in the effort to care for his family and to make it in the system. A co-founder of the group has co-authored (with a white feminist sociologist) a book entitled *Cool Pose,* elaborating, if inadvertently, a simplification of the material of our previously mentioned *Negro Digest* article of 1964, "The Frustrated Masculinity of the Negro Male."

The other group, naming itself "The Black Man Think Tank" — causing frequent calls from individuals, including the press, confusing it with The Black Think Tank — holds annually under the auspices of a major white university, a conference with an ostensibly heterosexual ambition, but appearing to excite the particular enthusiasm of homosexuals. This is not to denigrate homosexuals but to call attention to the profound black male *heterosexual* dilemma.

Within this atmosphere of silence and inaction, the announcement in recent months of Nation of Islam leader Louis Farrakhan's proposal to organize a million-strong black man march on Washington in the fall of this year appeared sufficient to arouse old FBI "COINTELPRO" tactics of disruption and division to face the faintly stirring black male.

So what are we to do? I can tell you one thing: the black woman is getting tired. She's losing her patience, tired of waiting on us. She's starting to wonder out loud if we can really pull this matter of black liberation off. The only thing stopping her from giving up on the black male altogether is she knows that, in a patriarchal society, a people cannot come to power and recognition until the moment that its males break out of their slumber and the psychic comfort of the symbolic matriarchal womb.

The black woman knows on some level, furthermore — and this is a thing that Frantz Fanon explained — that the oppressor works through the woman, wrenching her free from her customs and loyalties, winning her over to his values and, through her, to control the man. So, the more the black man tests the black woman's patience, the more she grows disenchanted and submissive to the propaganda of her "sisterhood" with Mrs. Anne — beginning with the once-controversial Michelle Wallace, who became the darling of *Ms.* magazine and white feminism when she wrote her strident late 1970s book, *The Black Macho and The Myth of the Super Black Woman.* Ms. Wallace explained to a *New York Times* reporter that she had written the book out of her anger over black men who turn their backs on her and her beautiful black sisters to marry white women instead or otherwise desert their family obligations.

But, while the black male is there with her, a black woman's commitment to keeping up with her girlfriends can hold his nose to the grindstone, enslaving him and her both to the high tech plantation, the corporation, unable to experiment with doing anything much for self. Anytime the black male steps out of the cocoon of conformity, he places her goals of assimilation and the quest for materialism immediately at stake.

It is necessary, then, for her part, that black women cease to demand that their own individual black mates be toms only to turn around and lambaste black males as a group for failing to confront the white man. Never mind what people say — I heard Minister Farrakhan when he said that, "if the black man does not rise, the white man will not fall."

Beyond that, brother, the ball is in your court, in your hands. Take it to the hoop. Start now to stay with your women and children. Cherish them, love them, protect them, nourish and nurture them. For, when it comes to the elevation of a people, the cementing of our future, they may be the most important thing that you will ever have. Be good to them.

Be strong, black man, be strong enough to be weak sometimes where your women and your children are involved. They are not your enemy, as you well know.

So come now, stop whimpering. Brother, it's too late to turn back now. Let us face the white man and his schemes, his diabolical system, head-on. It's freedomtime. It's nationtime. It's getting up time, time to get going, brotherman, time now for the black man to rise again, time now for the black man to get up out of his bed and walk.

Acknowledgments

Grateful aknowledgment is made for permission to reprint previously published poems from *Black Male/Female Relationships*.

The Black Think Tank. "Where Have You Gone" Copyright by Mari Evans, from p.18, Vol. 2, No. 1, 1980.

"If I Could Snap My Finger," Copyright by Njeri H. Nuru, from p. 18, Vol. 2, No. 1, 1980.

"Confessions of an Ex-Wife Beater," Copyright by Marvin X, from p. 20, 60, Year 2, No. 5, 1980.

"Calling All Black Men," Copyright by Marvin X, from Vol. 2, #1, 1981.